D0848743

DEFENSELESS

DEFENSELESS

COMMAND FAILURE AT PEARL HARBOR

JOHN W. LAMBERT
NORMAN POLMAR

MBI

First published in 2003 by Motorbooks International, an imprint of
MBI Publishing Company, Galtier Plaza, Suite 200, 380 Jackson Street,
St. Paul, MN 55101-3885 USA

© John W. Lambert and Norman Polmar, 2003

All rights reserved. With the exception of quoting brief passages for the purposes
of review, no part of this publication may be reproduced without prior written
permission from the Publisher.

The information in this book is true and complete to the best of our knowledge.
All recommendations are made without any guarantee on the
part of the author or Publisher, who also disclaim any liability incurred in
connection with the use of this data or specific details.

We recognize that some words, model names, and designations, for example,
mentioned herein are the property of the trademark holder. We use them for
identification purposes only. This is not an official publication.

Motorbooks International titles are also available at discounts in bulk quantity for
industrial or sales-promotional use. For details write to Special Sales Manager at
Motorbooks International Wholesalers & Distributors,
Galtier Plaza, Suite 200, 380 Jackson Street, St. Paul, MN 55101-3885 USA.

ISBN 0-7603-1739-9

On the front cover : (top) Lieutenant General Walter C. Short and Admiral
Husband E. Kimmel, the top military commanders in Hawaii at the time of the
attack. *National Archives* (bottom) The battleship *California* took several hits and
burned furiously while some crew members abandoned ship. *National Archives*

Edited by Steve Gansen and Leah Noel
Designed by Tom Heffron

Printed in the United States of America

Contents

"The first casualty when war comes is truth."

—Sen. Hiram Johnson in the United States Senate, 1917

Foreword

In the 1960s I began to research the history of a seemingly forgotten unit, The Seventh Air Force of World War II. Volumes on the other numbered U.S. air forces abound, but by little surfaced in the postwar years about the Seventh—the old Hawaiian Air Force. My efforts to chronicle the exploits of the Seventh's 15th Fighter Group led to a 25-year association with surviving members of the Hawaiian fighter fraternity. That research culminated in two volumes: *The Long Campaign: The History of the 15th Fighter Group*, (Sunflower Press), 1980; and *The Pineapple Air Force: Pearl Harbor to Tokyo*, (Phalanx Publishing), 1990.

Along the way, I was honored to attend several Seventh Fighter Command reunions. Some of the men had been present when the war began on Oahu and had served in campaigns across the Pacific that ultimately led to flying long-range missions to the Japanese home islands. They were mostly lieutenants when the war started, and those who survived were leading fighter groups and squadrons at war's end.

The old "Pineapples" as the Hawaiian vets called themselves, knew little or nothing of the international chess moves that triggered the Pacific War. But they all expressed a feeling that regardless of their valorous performance on that day and in the years that followed, they had been misused and poorly served by their superiors in Hawaii in the period leading up to 7 December 1941.

Few had an opportunity to testify before investigative panels about the failures that left them unprepared when the Japanese first attacked. The handful who were called to testify were "strongly urged" if not outright ordered to only offer information that was directly asked for, nothing more. Once the military careers of these men ended, they were ready to talk openly. In most cases, my interviews released a torrent of lingering resentment that the entire story behind the disaster had not been totally revealed to the public.

My good friend Norman Polmar contributed his extensive knowledge of history and naval matters to this book. Together, we uncovered information that is both new and unique, much of it gleaned from Pearl Harbor archives that investigators and legions of historians have either neglected or just plain misinterpreted. It is important to set the record straight.

After decades of official secrecy and rhetoric, Admiral Kimmel and General Short are on the verge of having the real truth permanently obscured and swept forever under the rug of revisionist history. Future scholars would be deprived of the hard facts leading up to the disaster: the not-so-pretty reality that Kimmel and Short were ultimately derelict in their duty, resulting in the greatest catastrophe in U.S. naval history.

Our efforts have taken on a new urgency in the past few years when the historical record seemed to have been permanently rewritten. The most dire example came down to politics filtering the truth through a rose-colored lens. In 1999, by a vote of 52 to 47, the U.S. Senate passed a resolution that cleared Kimmel and Short of their failures of command. The late Senator Strom Thurmond went so far as to call them "the final two victims of Pearl Harbor."

Over the years books by Kimmel-Short advocates have done their best to portray both men as innocent scapegoats. Some conspiracy theorists have even tried to blame Franklin Delano Roosevelt for baiting the Japanese into an attack and denying Hawaii the means to defend itself. This preposterous proposition is based on myths that remain widely circulated in this age of the Internet.

The real failure at Pearl Harbor was born out of the arrogance of senior Hawaiian officers who subtly resisted cooperation and refused to inform themselves on air defense technology and procedures. In the subsequent investigations, they dishonestly blamed each other and subordinates, even attempting to manipulate facts to justify their dereliction.

Our intention is not to review every issue related to the events of 7 December 1941 but review only those matters that related to the preparedness of the citadel of Oahu. The threat of an attack by the Japanese on the Pacific Fleet at Oahu had been a nightmare for the U.S. military since 1928, when it began war planning for such a scenario. Yet somehow, the senior on-scene commanders were caught completely unprepared when reality bore down on Oahu in the form of 350 Japanese carrier aircraft.

It is my greatest hope that this book will both lay the far-fetched myths to rest and add to the historic knowledge of that tragic event. And while it is not likely to sway the most devoted Kimmel-Short supporters, it may give those old Pineapples their due.

Those participants in the event who supplied information and permitted interviews are listed in Appendix I and in many cases their words are quoted. Endnotes are used to verify archival sources.

Norman Polmar and I are indebted to fellow historians Barrett Tillman, Mike Wenger, and Bob Cressman for their insights and suggestions; Barry Levenson for his legal perspective; and Steve Gansen at MBI Publishing Company for his encouragement, editing, and attempts to keep everyone on course.

—Jack Lambert

Introduction

7 December 1941: The Japanese navy launches a surprise air raid on the U.S. Pacific Fleet at its base in Pearl Harbor in Hawaii, sinking or heavily damaging 19 warships, destroying or damaging more than 340 navy and army aircraft, and killing more than 2,400 military and civilian personnel. This event plunged the United States into World War II and neutralized the U.S. Pacific Fleet, permitting the rapid Japanese conquest of Southeast Asia, the Philippines, and the Dutch East Indies.

The effort to determine the cause of this military disaster continues to this day. Unfortunately, the truth regarding the fundamental issue of Hawaii's preparedness and the failed defense of Oahu has been obscured, even by many knowledgeable military people.

No matter what misconceptions have come out of these investigations, know this: Admiral Husband E. Kimmel and Lieutenant General Walter C. Short, Hawaii's top commanders at the time of the attack, failed to employ available defenses that fateful day. But Kimmel and Short devotees, including many historians, believe almost religiously in a Washington, D.C–based conspiracy, contending that Kimmel and Short were scapegoats for President Franklin D. Roosevelt and others (see Appendix A for principals).

Roosevelt and Army Chief of Staff General George C. Marshall would never have risked the loss of the Pacific Fleet and Pearl Harbor's naval facilities for the mere pretext of America's entry into World War II. Nor could they have orchestrated such an elaborate failure even if they wanted to. It would have taken a conspiracy not of two men, but of thousands over several decades to pull off such a far-fetched scheme in perfect secrecy.

No such high treason led to the attack on Pearl Harbor. The reality is that the Hawaiian commanders were derelict in the following respects:

1. **They failed to search for the enemy, although specifically ordered to do so.**
2. **They failed to employ an operational Aircraft Warning Service to detect approaching aircraft and direct defending interceptors.**
3. **They failed to have the army interceptor force on alert.**
4. **They failed to establish inter- and intra-service cooperation on vital matters related to the defense of Oahu.**

Over the years, Kimmel and Short claimed that they had insufficient aircraft with which to conduct distant reconnaissance, when in fact ample aircraft were available for searches in what their commands had determined as the most critical sectors. Moreover, they failed to take into account the lessons of more than 10 years of annual U.S. fleet exercises in which carrier-based aircraft successfully made mock surprise attacks against Pearl Harbor and the Panama Canal, and they ignored the long-established war planning assumptions of a possible preemptive Japanese strike.

A series of eight post-attack investigations (see Appendix C) found fault with both the Hawaiian commanders and senior officials in Washington, but these did not go to the core of the failed defense for three reasons:

1. **Early hearings, held during the course of the war, were conducted in secret so as not to compromise military security.**
2. **Junior officers were reluctant to express themselves.**
3. **A lack of knowledge among the investigative panel members regarding military technology and operating procedures often frustrated the discovery of the true facts.**

The truth is that few citadels in modern history were better equipped to meet an anticipated attack or more sufficiently warned of impending peril. Hawaii had the capacity for at least a limited long-range reconnaissance of Oahu's sea approaches, and a state-of-the-art air defense system was in place and functional but unmanned.

When the lone Japanese float scout aircraft from the heavy cruiser *Chikuma* conducted its surveillance of Oahu, which began more than an hour prior to the planned air strike, radar detected it and reported the target to the Aircraft Warning Service's Fort Shafter Information Center as early as 06:41 A.M. Some 20 minutes later, radar units detected and reported the approach of the first wave of Japanese carrier aircraft, which at that point were 130 miles north of Oahu. Simultaneously, the U.S. destroyer *Ward* and a navy patrol bomber located and attacked a Japanese midget submarine near the Pearl Harbor entrance. For some reason, neither of these incidents stirred the Hawaiian military establishment.

In fact, months before the Japanese struck Oahu, the island's ranking army and navy airmen crafted a joint defense plan. It forecast an attack scenario that closely mirrored the 7 December strike and, based on incessant drills (see Appendix B), appeared to be thorough, sound, and workable. Its centerpiece was the Aircraft Warning Service (AWS), which would coordinate radar, fighter aircraft, and antiaircraft artillery.

Early in 1941, the army and navy studied and adopted the coordinated air defense system pioneered by Britain's Royal Air Force (RAF) in the 1940 Battle of Britain. America's fledgling Air Defense Command was established at Mitchel Field, Long Island, and army officers from Hawaii were among the first schooled at Mitchel in the process of detection, identification, and ground-controlled interception.

Indeed, there was a sense of urgency about Hawaii's defense in both Washington and Honolulu, caused by a belligerent Japan that had, within a relatively short period, emerged on the international stage as a great naval power.

Part I

The
Background to War

Chapter 1

War Planning

The Pacific Ocean sprawls nearly 7,000 nautical miles from the West Coast of the United States to the mainland of Asia. This expanse of water is speckled with small islands and little else. For most of its first century, the United States military focused its attention on its Atlantic neighbors, the source of America's founding immigrants and its major trading partners. Except for random explorations, the growing nation largely ignored the Pacific. The Spanish-American conflict of 1898, however, and the subsequent conquest of the Philippines propelled the United States into the role of a Pacific Ocean power out of necessity. Military planners in Washington were forced to consider ways of defending the country's distant Pacific possessions, which in 1941 included the Philippines, Guam, and Hawaii.

Japan, an insular, feudal society, had been slow in entering the empire-building business. But once Japan's industrial revolution began late in the nineteenth century, the lust of this small island nation for land and natural resources rivaled that of the long-established

European powers. Japan's first modern foreign adventure was its 1894 war with China, where a Japanese victory established its foothold on the Asian mainland. The Russo-Japanese War of 1904–1905 resulted in a crushing defeat for Tsar Nicholas II's land and sea forces, giving Japan control of Manchuria and confirming its hold on Korea. At the outset of World War I, in typical historical irony, the Japanese sided with the Allies, seizing Germany's Shantung Peninsula enclave in China.

A post-World War I League of Nations began mandating control of the remote central Pacific islands to various victors, and it consented to Japan's confiscation of the remote, and seemingly worthless, German Micronesia. However, this concession further extended Japan's Pacific perimeter, which had grown by thousands of square miles in the span of only four decades. It also provided the prerequisite for its strategic vision of Asia. [1]

Japan's army threatened both China and Soviet Siberia in the 1920s but backed down due to international condemnation and the refusal of Japan's own democratic assembly to fund the army's initiatives. However, after of its victory in the Russo-Japanese War and its support of the Allies in World War I, Japan could not be denied a place at the Washington Naval Conference of 1921–1922. While the major powers of the day—the United States, Great Britain, France, Italy, and Japan—had the bold desire to stop a warship construction race by establishing "ratio formulas" for the possession of capital ships in each nation's fleet, the real effect of this toothless gathering was to create Japan as the world's third largest naval power.[2] Meanwhile, Japan simply ignored the treaty's call for status quo with regard to naval bases and fortifications in the Pacific.

The statesmen who had held sway in Japan for nearly a decade were soon rendered impotent. In 1931 the Japanese army, independent of its government, created an incident in Manchuria and moved to occupy the resource-rich country. China, the United States, and the League of Nations objected, but had no real capacity to expel the invaders. The success of this invasion emboldened Japanese militarists to stage a coup, resulting in the decline of democratic government and the ascendancy of a military clique. What followed was the China Incident of 1937, a pretext for war against a hapless nation.

The creeping expansion of Japan in the Pacific had worried U.S. military strategists as early as 1905. By the late 1930s, there was no other significant military power in the vast Pacific other than Great Britain. With America's stake in the Philippines, the military planners started to look to the west and attempted to formulate a response to what many already saw as an inevitable outcome. The assumption was that despite a past history of amicable relations, Japan would succumb to its aggressive nature and its need for raw materials and attempt to dominate the Far East.

The earliest U.S. military plan for such aggression was drawn up at the turn of the century. It was unbelievably complex, with scenarios requiring the U.S. Atlantic Fleet to proceed to the Pacific via the Indian Ocean or around South America via the Straits of Magellan. Not until the 1914 completion of the Panama Canal could fleets readily shift from one coast to the other. Still, the distance from the East Coast of the United States to the Philippines via the canal was a formidable 11,000 nautical miles.

U.S. war planning was not a science but an art. No presidential or congressional mandates to plan for war in the Pacific existed, and the state department was outright disdainful of the practice as being undiplomatic. Thus it was a task largely undertaken in secret from the rest of government. The post-World War I U.S. Army, a scant force never more than 150,000, was largely indifferent to the matter. Navy leaders simply accepted that providing for such a contingency was part of their job. The war planners, wary of potential political problems, devised a color code for nations: blue was for the United States, red for Great Britain, black for Germany, and orange for Japan.

War Plan Orange first came into being in 1907. The resounding defeat of Russian naval forces by Japan in 1905 had startled most Western military planners. Japanese armies attacking the Asian mainland were a remote concern, but no one had previously considered the extension of Japanese power through use of naval forces. The war planning process was not only ongoing, but a Japan versus the United States scenario was played as a continuing game at the Naval War College at Newport, Rhode Island. On the basis of advancing technology and economic considerations, war plans were constantly being modified and updated. But the one constant in the strategy to contain Japanese aggression and rescue the Philippines was the use of Oahu as a base.

Invasion of Japan and its island bases was also a scenario considered by war planners. However, the most likely scenario was an aggressive thrust by Japan against the Philippines or other western Pacific regions that would compel the United States to intercede. In such an event, Japan would have the shorter supply lines and the U.S. fleet would be obliged to deal with a crisis some 6,000 miles from California. Hence, the Hawaiian Islands, Oahu with its Pearl Harbor in particular, became an absolutely vital logistics base for the Pacific Fleet. [3]

Manila was the only location in the Philippines with a suitable deep-water port that could provide the necessary refueling, supply, and repair facilities for the U.S. Navy. However, budgetary or political concerns led to a modest naval ship presence in the western Pacific. Even if the construction of such repair and refueling facilities had been undertaken, a fleet advancing from the continental United States could not accomplish the transpacific crossing without refueling.

Oahu, 2,200 nautical miles from the U.S. mainland, was the key to American control of the central Pacific and the logical jumping-off point for either a sortie to the Philippines (albeit a 3,000-nautical mile marathon from Oahu) or a foray to bring the Japanese fleet to a decisive battle. Midway, Wake, and Guam Islands were stepping stones along the way, but with few funded facilities for the fleet, they became viewed primarily as bases for potential air reconnaissance.

By the 1930s, a very small U.S. Navy squadron was based at Manila—the Asiatic Fleet—as a token force. But no major repair or refueling facilities were in the Far East, as the nagging concern was that the Philippines might be quickly overrun regardless of a naval response. The logical focal point for the Pacific Fleet became Pearl Harbor. In the event of war with Japan, the U.S. Pacific Fleet would advance from the U.S. West Coast to Hawaii, refuel, and then proceed to the western Pacific.

In accordance with the terms of the Washington Naval Conference, the United States and Great Britain had scrapped many old warships, and treaty and budget restraints allowed for the construction of only a few new ones for their multi-ocean fleets. However, the Japanese steadily increased their military expenditures to a disproportionate percentage of their national economy. While the Naval Conferences of 1930, 1935, and 1936 were marked by arguments for naval parity, Japan embarked on an ambitious warship construction plan with a heavy emphasis on super battleships, aircraft carriers, and lesser warships. Before the treaty expired, the Japanese gave notice of their intention to terminate participation. Thus, on the eve of World War II, the Japanese fleet was more powerful than the combined Allied Pacific fleets. [4]

Japan achieved this military prominence seemingly overnight by becoming an industrial and maritime power with the capacity to wage war and an inclination toward aggression. It was an astonishing transition for the feudal kingdom, which Commodore Matthew Perry had first opened to the Western world in 1853, revealing a picture of an isolated, backward agrarian society.

The Japanese navy had created war plans that were the mirror image of U.S. plans. According to David Evans and Mark Peattie in their study *Kaigun*:

> By World War I the naval staffs in both Tokyo and Washington centered their study of a Pacific war on two common assumptions: That Japan would conduct offensive operations against the Philippines at the outset of any such conflict, and that the United States would move a battle fleet westward across the Pacific to come to the aid of the American garrisons and naval units there.[5]

Thus, the decisive fleet engagement had become an imperative in the war plans of both Japan and America.

As war erupted throughout Europe in 1939, U.S. war planners were faced with new and perplexing problems. The British fleet had its hands full in the Atlantic, Mediterranean, and North Sea. The U.S. Navy's Pacific Fleet sent warships and aircraft to reinforce the Atlantic Fleet, to conduct "neutrality patrols," and to escort merchant ships in the U-boat infested waters of the Atlantic.

Because of the U-boat menace, which seemed to threaten the very survival of Great Britain, and with the success of Germany in the early stages of conflict on the European continent, War Plan Orange (Japan) was subject to constant revision. The old plan gave way to color variations that were labeled Rainbow. However, from 1907 until America's formal entry into World War II, there had been only one enemy in the Pacific war strategy planning process. The solitary potential antagonist was Japan, and the only conceivable threat to the Philippines and Hawaii would come from the Japanese navy.

War Plan Rainbow assumed that Japan would make an aggressive move toward the oil and other strategic riches of the Netherlands' East Indies and British Malaya. Japan could not hope to do so with a strong U.S. military force on its eastern flank in the Philippines. Thus, U.S. planners set forth scenarios for the Pacific Fleet to sortie to the defense of the Philippines via Hawaii, with Oahu being an absolutely essential refueling stop. It followed in U.S. military thinking that Oahu was, therefore, subject to being neutralized by a pre-emptive Japanese naval attack. [6]

Indeed, from 1928 onward, beginning with the pioneer U.S. aircraft carrier *Langley*, the fleet had practiced surprise air attacks against Pearl Harbor and the Panama Canal as part of the annual fleet exercises. Not until Fleet Problem XX in 1939 was there a major fleet exercise in the Atlantic. Senior navy and, to a significant degree, army aviators on active service in 1941 had participated in these annual exercises, or at least knew of the regular—and successful— carrier air strikes against Pearl Harbor and the Panama Canal.

A surprise air attack on Hawaii, which was a U.S. territory until well after World War II, by the Japanese fleet had been forecast in a Nostradamus-like report to the U.S. War Department by Brigadier General "Billy" Mitchell after his 1924 Asian tour. [7]

War Department strategy in the Pacific increasingly saw Pearl Harbor as an imperiled "fortress." The army chief of intelligence in 1941, Major General Sherman Miles, who was the army's Hawaiian Department operations officer from 1929 to 1932 and in charge of the Hawaiian War Plans Division in Washington from 1934 to 1938, stated:

> During all those seven years that the defense plans
> were under my supervision, or certainly with my

very intimate knowledge, a surprise attack by the
Japanese on Hawaii, made with little or no warning,
was a basic consideration in the defense plans. . . . An
attack on Hawaii was inherent in any war in which
we might become involved with Japan. [8]

Just as U.S. war plans focused on a sortie to engage the Japanese
fleet, the Japanese navy calculated the need for a decisive engagement with the U.S. fleet. To defend against this contingency, U.S. war
planners assumed that the Japanese navy had drafted a strategy to
engage the United States, with Pearl Harbor being a likely starting
point for hostilities.

The Japanese Imperial Navy had considered the U.S. Navy its sole
antagonist since 1909. Commander Mitsuo Fuchida, who led the
attack on Pearl Harbor, recalled that in 1921 when he entered Japan's
Eta Jima naval academy, "it was said that the potential enemy is
America." [9]

The Japanese Imperial Naval War College had "played" at a Pearl
Harbor attack from the mid-1930s. With President Roosevelt shifting
the Pacific Fleet from the West Coast to Hawaii in April 1940,
Japanese ambitions posed a real threat, and the theoretical attack on
Oahu became a compellingly necessary, if not daring, strategy. [10]

The U.S. Navy had conducted fleet exercises with a mock strike
on Pearl Harbor by aircraft as far back as 1928. On 17 May, the
Langley launched its aircraft against Oahu. Similar mock raids from
U.S. Navy carriers were conducted periodically, as an aspect of
planned war games. [11]

In a postwar interview, Vice Admiral Shigeru Fukudome, chief of
staff to the commander in chief of the Combined Fleet when the war
began, reflected on Japanese strategy:

Now, with the U.S. fleet already advanced to its Hawaiian base, it could readily continue to the Western Pacific, thus creating a definite threat to Japan. As long as it remained at its Hawaiian base, it created a strategic situation incomparably more tense and threatening to the Japanese than when it was based on the Pacific Coast. [12]

President Roosevelt had ordered the Pacific Fleet to remain at Pearl Harbor as a deterrent. The Japanese accepted it as such and prepared to deal with this strategic menace. Prior to their early 1941 assignments to Hawaii, both Admiral Kimmel and General Short were briefed on war plan assumptions and scenarios, as they would later testify.

1. Willard Price, *Japan's Islands of Mystery*, pp. 20–25.
2. Paul S. Dull, *A Battle History of the Imperial Japanese Navy (1941–1945)*, p. 4.
3. Edward S. Miller, *War Plan Orange*, p. 21.
4. Samuel E. Morison, *History of United States Naval Operations in World War II, Vol. III*, p. 58.
5. David C. Evans and Mark K. Peattie, *Kaigun*, p. 189.
6. Joint Congressional Committee on Pearl Harbor, Part 27, p. 838.
7. Burke Davis, *The Billy Mitchell Affair*, pp. 170–175.
8. Joint Congressional Committee, Part 27, pp. 819–821.
9. Mitsuo Fuchida and Masatake Okumiya, *Midway, The Battle That Doomed Japan*, p. 11.
10. David C. Evans, *The Japanese Navy in World War II*, p. 8.
11. Deck log, USS *Langley*, National Archives, RG 24.
12. David C. Evans, *The Japanese Navy in World War II*, p. 9.

Chapter 2

The Path to
Pearl Harbor

The world press and the yet-to-be-defunct League of Nations con-
demned Japan for the carnage in its all-out war against China,
which began in July 1937. Subsequent Japanese occupation of
Hainan Island and the then-irrelevant Spratly Islands, which had
been claimed by France, provided further evidence of Japan's expan-
sionist policies. Brutal newsreel scenes and reports coming out of
China, incidents against foreign nationals, and the sinking of the U.S.
gunboat *Panay* on the Yangtze River on 12 December 1937 inflamed
American public opinion against Japan. Veteran Japanese diplomats
attempted to assure Washington of their willingness to negotiate
solutions, but the Japanese government, dominated by the military,
showed little remorse and grew increasingly arrogant.

The American public and congress, although angered by Japan's
actions, still retained the memory of World War I casualties from
only 20 years ago. Americans were also preoccupied with the last
stages of the Great Depression. Both were factors that fostered an
isolationist mood. Germany's capricious acts preceding its invasion

of Poland in September 1939 and the subsequent declaration of war by Britain and France only reinforced America's fear of foreign entanglements. The public felt safe behind the Atlantic and Pacific Ocean barriers.

The Roosevelt administration and the military establishment were increasingly nervous over Japan's aggression in the West and the U-boat campaign underway in the Atlantic. Shaking off an economic recession, America was unprepared for war, much less a war across two oceans. When the Germans plunged through the lowlands of Holland and Belgium and forced an armistice on France barely a month later in May 1940, U.S. government officials feared for Britain's survival.

The combination of German military successes in Europe, the implications for the Dutch East Indies and French Indochina, and Japan's heightened belligerency caused alarm in Washington over the possible breakout of war in the Pacific, triggering the first of many Hawaiian alerts. [1]

In September 1940, Japan joined Germany and Italy in a tripartite pact that became known as the Axis. Each Axis power pledged to support the other in the event of an attack by a nation not already involved in the European war. This provided Japan with some protection from the United States and the Soviet Union. A year earlier, in 1939, the Japanese had executed another of their infamous "border incidents," this time with the Soviet Union. It took place on the Nomonhon River in northern Manchuria. After initial success, Japanese forces were soundly thrashed and sent back across the border by the Red Army. If the Japanese army intended to invade China and expand its conquests to the south, the army could ill afford a belligerent Soviet army on its northern flank. Hitler took care of that threat with his June 1941 invasion of the U.S.S.R. German victory over France had provided an opportunity for Japan to make a strategic move on China's southern flank. With the connivance of Hitler, Vichy France acceded to a Japanese occupation of Indochina in August 1940.

The Japanese army, having seized most of coastal China, compelled surviving Chinese armies to withdraw into their vast hinterland where the Japanese were presented with progressive problems of transport and supply. More important to long-range Japanese goals, Indochina gave them air bases in proximity to British Malaya and brought them closer to the Netherlands' East Indies.

Washington protested Japan's aggressive actions for several years, yet seemingly without impact. Then token trade sanctions were threatened, which also failed to influence Japanese behavior. Finally, between July and September 1940, President Roosevelt embargoed shipments to Japan of high-octane gasoline, fuel oil, aircraft parts and engines, certain minerals and chemicals, and scrap metals. This action was intended to compel Japan to retract from its conquests. But instead it only emboldened Japan's militaristic stance.

Lacking its own oil resources in appreciable quantities, Japan had imported heavily from the United States, the Persian Gulf, and Peru. Most of this oil fueled its war machine. The embargo, however, forced Japan's hand, and the land of the rising sun embarked on a course of action that would capture the resources of Malaya and the East Indies by sweeping aside local British and Dutch forces. Hard pressed by the German successes of 1941 in North Africa and the Mediterranean, as well as the need to provide arms to the beleaguered Soviet Union, Britain could ill afford to spare military forces to reinforce its Far East holdings. Holland had been overrun by German legions, and its government, which was in exile in London, could provide no assistance to its small army and navy in the East Indies. The only uncertain factor in Japan's Southeast Asia strategy was the potential military response of the United States.

Wary of Japanese intentions long before instituting the oil embargo, President Roosevelt had sent the Pacific Fleet on maneuvers from its home base at San Pedro, California, to Hawaii in April 1940. The navy conducted exercises well west of the 180th meridian and then returned to Pearl Harbor. In May, at Roosevelt's direction, Admiral Harold R. Stark, the chief of naval operations, ordered the fleet to stay put. When the fleet commander Admiral James O. Richardson asked why, he was advised that the fleet in that position posed a deterrent to the Japanese.

Admiral Richardson was, however, concerned regarding Oahu's limited fleet support facilities, its lack of air defense, and the potential for a torpedo attack against his ships at Pearl Harbor. He journeyed to Washington in October 1940 in an attempt to get the order rescinded and campaigned for return of the fleet to California. [2]

Rear Admiral Claude Bloch, the 63-year-old commandant of Hawaii's 14th Naval District and a former U.S. fleet commander, also complained about the situation in a letter of 30 December 1940 to the chief of naval operations. He detailed the navy's concerns regarding inadequate army defenses (antiaircraft artillery, fighters, and bombers) to protect against a hostile surprise attack. Richardson supported Bloch with an endorsement to the letter. [3]

For these expressions of displeasure with the status of the fleet, Oahu's air defense, and President Roosevelt's Pacific strategy, Richardson was removed from command and replaced by Rear Admiral Husband E. Kimmel, a 1904 graduate of the U.S. Naval Academy. When he relieved Richardson on 1 February 1941, Kimmel was given the rank of admiral. His naval career had been highly successful: He was aide to Assistant Secretary of the Navy Franklin D. Roosevelt in 1915 and then served in U.S. battleships in European waters during the last year of World War I. He had commanded several ships, including the battleship *New York*. At the time of his appointment to head the Pacific Fleet, the 58-year-old Kimmel commanded the battle force's three light cruiser divisions at Pearl Harbor and thus was promoted over a number of more senior flag officers.

While Richardson had been commander in chief of the U.S. fleet, Kimmel became commander in chief of the Pacific Fleet and Admiral Ernest J. King became commander in chief of the Atlantic Fleet when the fleet was reorganized. The reorganization reflected the increasing role of the navy in the Atlantic, which included carrying out neutrality patrols and actively supporting the British battle against U-boats.

The Pearl Harbor change of command was held on board the fleet flagship *Pennsylvania*. However, two months later, in April 1941, Kimmel moved his staff from the crowded *Pennsylvania* ashore to the second deck of the headquarters building at the Pearl Harbor submarine base. From his new offices, Kimmel could look down at the submarine piers and out across Pearl Harbor to Ford Island and Battleship Row—where the fleet's dreadnoughts would moor when in port. On the far side of Ford Island was the aircraft carrier anchorage, while the island's airfield was home to four squadrons of PBY flying boats and numerous utility aircraft. When carriers were in port, their squadrons also came to roost on Ford Island.

Immediately after the change of command, Richardson and Kimmel prepared a joint estimate of the Pacific situation based on War Plan Rainbow. This 25 January 1941 letter to Washington presumed that war with Japan was imminent, and again, the navy represented that army defenses for Pearl Harbor were inadequate to meet a surprise attack. [4]

Just a few days later, on 7 February, Major General Walter C. Short relieved Major General Charles D. Herron at the army's Hawaiian Department. With this routine change of command, the second of the two primary figures in one of America's greatest military disasters was in place.

1. Joint Congressional Committee, Part 15, p. 1929.

2. Ibid., Part 1, pp. 274–282.

3. Navy Court of Inquiry, Part 33, Exhibit 28, pp. 1193–96.

4. Ibid., Exhibit 70, pp. 1349–51.

Chapter 3

The
Hawaiian Buildup

In the era before the U.S. Department of Defense combined its forces, the Hawaiian military establishment had its own complex command system. Admiral Kimmel had command of the Pacific Fleet, and Rear Admiral Claude C. Bloch was responsible for navy facilities ashore as commander of the 14th Naval District. On his last tour of duty before retirement, Bloch was subordinate to Kimmel. The army's Hawaiian Department was responsible for the defense of Oahu and the outlying Hawaiian Islands, with the Pacific Fleet being considered the Hawaiian Department's "tenant." Short (promoted to lieutenant general with the new assignment) commanded all army ground and air forces in the Hawaiian Islands, a force whose strength would total more than 42,000 officers and enlisted men (including Air Force personnel) just prior to the attack of 7 December 1941.

Although not a West Pointer, Short had risen steadily in the army. He received his commission after graduation from the University of Illinois and served as a junior officer in a variety of posts. He was in France during World War I and, in the postwar years, attended the

Army War College, serving in a variety of staff and command assignments. The 61-year-old Short was an infantryman by trade and was recognized in the army for his skill in training troops.

His Hawaiian Department ground forces consisted of more than 33,000 soldiers, infantry, artillery, and support units. Of these, 1,200 were posted to other islands in the Hawaiian group. The bulk of the army, which included 10,000 members of the 24th and 25th divisions, was stationed on Oahu, centrally located at Schofield Barracks no more than an hour away from any of the likely invasion beaches. An amphibious landing on Oahu, at the limited beaches that were suitable, could be a costly affair for an aggressor. At some of the more likely landing sites, like Waikiki, coastal artillery was already in place.

Short's air commander was 58-year-old Major General Frederick L. Martin, a man personally selected by the Army Air Corps chief, Major General Harold H. "Hap" Arnold. Arnold had sent Martin to Hawaii with the explicit charge of improving its air defense. Soon after Martin's arrival in November 1940, he established the 14th Pursuit Wing at Wheeler Field (Pursuit was a term that was later dropped in favor of fighter in the naming of these units). The bomber command resided at Hickam Field, adjacent to the Pearl Harbor naval base, and had an assortment of under-strength units. All army aviation units in the army's Hawaiian Department were officially designated as the Hawaiian Air Force.

The pursuit wing's subordinate combat unit, the 18th Pursuit Group, had been part of the Hawaiian scene for several years, growing slowly from one to three squadrons. It was equipped with Curtiss P-36 Hawk fighters of recent vintage and Boeing P-26 fighters, which were open-cockpit, fixed-landing gear dinosaurs that were obsolete by any standard. A second pursuit group, the 15th, was established on 1 December 1940, albeit short of men and without aircraft.

Brigadier General Howard C. Davidson arrived to command the newly formed 14th Pursuit Wing and oversee its growth.

Short immediately began to lobby Washington for additional troops, but primarily he sought aircraft, antiaircraft artillery, and air defense radar to provide suitable warning of an attack. He was advised that equipment would be forthcoming as soon as funding, production, and priority permitted. America, "the arsenal of democracy" as it was termed, was not yet engaged in World War II but was furiously attempting to shore up its own anemic military while also supplying Great Britain with arms. Although determined not to become involved in the war in Europe, the U.S. government was alarmed at the crisis facing the British, and armaments for Britain were a first priority. Officials in Washington also had gnawing awareness of the Pacific menace posed by Japan.

In a 7 February 1941 letter from Secretary of War Henry L. Stimson to Secretary of the Navy Frank Knox, Stimson discussed the impending dispatch of more P-36 aircraft and pilot reinforcements from the mainland to Hawaii. However, he assured Knox of the early shipment of the new Curtiss P-40 Tomahawk and also explained to him that the goal, based on available production, was to get Hawaii's ultimate strength to 148 fighters. He wrote: "The Hawaiian Department is the best equipped of all our overseas departments and continues to hold a high priority for the completion of its projected defenses because of the importance of giving full protection to the fleet."

With regard to the Aircraft Warning Service radar units, Stimson went on to state that the equipment had been ordered and would be delivered in June. [1]

In a February 1941 letter to General Short, Chief of Staff General Marshall reiterated Stimson's message and also disclosed some intelligence about the superiority of a new Japanese fighter that had appeared in China—the Mitsubishi A6M Zero. He also pleaded with Short to make Admiral Kimmel understand the competing demands of various war zones, including the Philippines, and Washington's attempts to prioritize and ration scarce equipment. He concluded with:

> Please keep clearly in mind in all of your negotiations that our mission is to protect the base and the naval concentrations, and that purpose should be made clearly apparent to Admiral Kimmel. I accentuate this because I found yesterday, for example . . . that old army-navy feuds, engendered from fights over appropriation, . . . still persist in confusing issues of national defense. We must be completely impersonal in these matters, at least so far as our own nerves and irritations are concerned. Fortunately, and happily, I might say, [Admiral Harold] Stark and I are on the most intimate personal basis, and that relationship has enabled us to avoid many serious difficulties. [2]

In January 1941, only 36 Army Air Corps fighter aircraft were available for the defense of Oahu, 19 of which were Curtiss P-36s. The rest of the aircraft were the obsolete Boeing P-26. Drawing fighters from two stateside units at Hamilton Field in California and Selfridge Field in Michigan, General Marshall freed another 30 P-36s and their pilots for transfer to Hawaii. The navy ferried the short-range fighters from San Diego on board the carrier *Enterprise*. They were flown off the flight deck near Oahu on 21 February 1941. Thus, with 60-plus aircraft, the 15th and 18th Pursuit Groups were slightly better equipped. [3]

The deficiency was further rectified in March 1941 when 55 factory-fresh P-40B fighters were shipped to Oahu. They were followed by additional B and a few C models. The Tomahawk had a top speed of 352 miles per hour, compared to 314 miles per hour for the P-36, and mounted six machine guns—four .30-caliber in the wings and a pair of .50-caliber in the nose—while the older P-36 Hawk fighters had only two machine guns. Overall, the P-40 was a technological leap forward. The same aircraft, in the hands of the Chinese-sponsored American volunteer group known as Chennault's Flying Tigers, would go into action at the end of 1941 and perform admirably against the Japanese.

In March 1941 the two top airmen in the Hawaiian military structure, Major General Martin and Rear Admiral Bellinger, reviewed the capacity of the air defense of Oahu and the Pearl Harbor naval base. Martin was the commander of the army's Hawaiian Air Force, and Rear Admiral Patrick N. L. Bellinger, in a Byzantine navy command structure, worked both under and outside of Admiral Bloch. Bellinger, who graduated from the naval academy in 1907, had served on both battleships and submarines before taking flight training. He became a naval aviator of some distinction after he flew a scouting aircraft during the Mexican campaign of 1914 and subsequently was involved in the navy's first attempted transatlantic crossing with flying boats. In Hawaii, the 56-year-old Bellinger wore several hats, including commander of the Hawaiian-based patrol wings. He also commanded whatever land-based aircraft were available on Oahu, including carrier planes when ashore. Working in complete harmony, Martin and Bellinger submitted a report to their superiors and to those in Washington a month later.

With War Plan Rainbow as a background, the Martin-Bellinger Report of 31 March 1941 first made an estimate of the potential risk of war, noting deterioration in relations between the United States and

Japan and the Japanese proclivity for hostile action without any formal declaration of war. The report forecast that possible enemy action against Oahu would take the form of a surprise air and submarine attack. It followed with an assessment of the air defense situation and provided a framework for joint operations both in scouting, interception, and bombing strikes against enemy forces. The entire basis for the report was an assumption that a Japanese carrier task force would attack Hawaii at dawn, launching from within 300 miles of Oahu. The report further forecast that the surprise attack could be delivered despite any long-range air reconnaissance by Hawaiian air units. [4]

According to the Martin-Bellinger report, the army had primary responsibility for the air defense of Oahu. It was to provide an air raid warning system, and the interceptors were required to repel an attack. Navy fighters ashore were to be inventoried daily, and the Hawaiian Air Force was to be notified of the number present and available to be dispatched as additional interceptors. Distant patrol was the responsibility of the navy, with the army's 18th Bombardment Wing supplying any of its "excess" aircraft that had long-range reconnaissance capability. The navy would be responsible for an attack on an enemy naval fleet, and army bombers would be available to augment that strike force. The Martin-Bellinger report was made as an annex to the Joint Coastal Frontier Defense Plan, which had been the operational basis for Hawaii's defense for several years. [5]

The Martin-Bellinger plan was comprehensive and seemingly a bulwark against air attack. However, it lacked some essential elements: unity of command, sufficient reconnaissance aircraft, and personnel. Since it was based on cooperation, the question of who would call the shots was left for a declaration by some higher authority. It had to be "vitalized" in the words of Lieutenant Commander Logan Ramsey, the Patrol Wing 2 operations officer. He and his superior, Bellinger, assumed that a call to arms would come from Admiral Bloch. [6]

Long before the plan had been drafted, Bellinger had been clamoring for more long-range patrol aircraft. The primary task of the navy patrol wings was to scout ahead of the fleet when it was at sea, detecting hostile submarines and surface forces. To fulfill that obligation, as well as patrol the approaches to Oahu for enemy surface and submarine units, Bellinger asked for 170 to 200 Consolidated PBY-5, Catalina twin-engine flying boats to replace his aging earlier model PBYs. This number of flying boats would permit a daily 700-mile search over 240 degrees of the compass, he calculated. Despite the heavy demands for these Catalinas in the Atlantic and other areas, Bellinger had received 60 of the PBY-5s by December 1941. Still short of his overall needs, he had a total of 81 of the invaluable Catalinas on 7 December 1941. [7]

Martin also sought to acquaint Washington with the continuing shortage of aircraft to provide what he considered minimal air defense requirements. In a 20 August 1941 assessment to Major General Arnold, Martin asked for a force of 180 long-range, four-engine Boeing B-17 Flying Fortress bombers to sufficiently search 360 degrees around the island of Oahu to a distance of 600 miles and still provide a ready reserve of strike aircraft. Since the world inventory of B-17s at that time was just 148 aircraft and many were being sent to beef up the Philippine air force, Martin's request could not be honored. [8]

In December 1941 Martin would have just 12 B-17Ds, six of which were fully operational. However, the Hawaiian Air Force was not lacking other multi-engine aircraft with significant long-range reconnaissance capability. Along with its handful of B-17s, it had three dozen bombers, mostly Douglas B-18 Bolos, with an operating radius of 400 to 500 miles depending on bomb load.

General Short also diligently pursued the requirement of more antiaircraft artillery. In March 1941, he complained to General

Marshall that he had sufficient three-inch heavy batteries but too few 37mm and .50-caliber automatic weapons. By December, his light antiaircraft artillery had been augmented. His heavy antiaircraft artillery numbered 98 three-inch guns, 76 of which were mobile. These batteries, which surrounded Pearl Harbor, were largely assigned to southern Oahu, between Fort Ruger and the Marine base at Ewa. Many were in the 16 new SCR-268 radar gun directors. [9] The Marines at Ewa provided an additional eight three-inch antiaircraft guns. [10] Coupled with the numerous light and heavy antiaircraft guns on fleet warships moored at Pearl Harbor, this mass of antiaircraft artillery, if were it manned and coordinated, had the potential to create a deadly screen of flak against hostile air attack.

On the advice of his air officers, General Short sought approval and funding for new airfields so that his aircraft units could be dispersed and bunkers could be used to protect his fighters at Wheeler Field, home of the 14th Pursuit Wing. The existing Bellows Field, on the east coast of Oahu, was improved, and a beach landing strip at Haleiwa, on the north coast, was in operation by December 1941. The bunker project progressed rapidly, and by December, 85 revetments were scattered in an arc around the south and eastern perimeter of Wheeler Field and were capable of protecting 109 aircraft. [11]

The all-important mobile air search radar arrived in Honolulu, as General Marshall had promised, on 4 August 1941. The technological wonder of its day, it also was being installed on several U.S. Navy warships. Radar, operating in conjunction with fighters and antiaircraft batteries, could provide the cornerstone of Oahu's air defense.

1. Joint Congressional Committee on Pearl Harbor, Part 14, Exhibit 10, p. 1003.
2. Ibid., Part 15, Exhibit 53, p. 1601.
3. Deck log, *Enterprise*, National Archives, RG 24.
4. Joint Congressional Committee on Pearl Harbor, Part 15, Exhibit 44, pp. 1433–1440.
5. Ibid., pp. 1434–1445.
6. Navy Court of Inquiry, Part 32, p. 436.
7. Roberts Commission, Part 24, Exhibit 6, p. 1367.
8. Army Pearl Harbor Board, Part 28, pp. 979-980.
9. Roberts Commission, Part 25, Exhibits 90 and 91.
10. Hart Inquiry, Part 26, p. 504.
11. Roberts Commission, Exhibit 89, Part 25.

Chapter 4

Oahu's Aircraft Warning Service

The U.S. military's ability to detect and repel an air attack depended upon an improved defense of the island bastion Oahu. With the advent of search radar, an Aircraft Warning Service (AWS) center began to take shape at Oahu's Fort Shafter. It was patterned after the prototype operation centers already built in New York and Boston. None other than Air Vice Marshal Hugh Dowding, who had directed Royal Air Force defenses in the Battle of Britain, inspected these U.S. centers and applied his imprimatur on them.

A combination of army personnel from the Signal Corps and Air Corps (the latter being designated Army Air Forces in June 1941) assembled the Oahu system over the summer of 1941. The key apparatus was radar, a new and highly secret device that the British had employed to good use, but was a strange new technology to the U.S. military.

In the summer of 1941, six SCR-270B radar sets arrived in Hawaii. These mobile, trailer-mounted, gas generator–powered units were enclosed in an operating van and a generator van. The U.S. Park Service caused initial delays regarding the location of radar sites, which had to be set up on prominent heights. However, by November the units were eventually located at Kaena Point, Opana Point, Kawailoa, Kaaawa, Koko Head, and Fort Shafter (See map No. 1). Roads were cut to the more remote locations, and then telephone lines were strung. In some cases, crude army field telephones were used until telephone company lines could be established.

The Army Signal Corps developed Hawaii's early SCR-270B mobile radar, which was then manufactured by Westinghouse. The antenna array resembled a giant bed spring and was adjusted by the operator, but it did not rotate continuously like modern radar. The operator aimed the antenna at various sectors and scanned for a target against which the radiated waves would echo back on the oscilloscope. After making contact with a target, the operator could then adjust or fine-tune the set for a better image. The refined image gave the operator an estimate of distance to the target. The SCR-270B had a theoretical range of 150 miles. A radar technician would then view the base ring for an azimuth bearing that would show the relative direction of the target from the radar site. Early radar could only detect objects, not readily identify them. It also could not determine altitude. The radar contact, or echo, reflected back to the radar station as an indistinct object on the oscilloscope. The echo could be any one of the following: ground clutter (the island of Kauai was visible some 90 miles northwest of Oahu), a ship, an aircraft, or flight of aircraft. The difference between aircraft and the other images was that an aircraft would noticeably move. After finding a target that seemed to move like one or more aircraft, the radar operator telephoned that data to the information center for plotting.

The information center was both the terminus of the radar network and the operational control point for Oahu's air defense. It was located in a temporary wooden structure in a Fort Shafter tunnel. Many phone lines had to be installed from the information center to all the services that had a "business" relationship with the Aircraft Warning Service. These included the 14th Pursuit Wing, 18th Bomb Wing, army antiaircraft and searchlights, navy patrol wing headquarters, 14th Naval District, civil aviation, and civil defense.

The information center building was an amphitheater with a huge plotting table in a lower pit depicting Oahu and the surrounding islands. The balcony above contained desks and telephones for officers of army pursuit, army bombers, navy shore-based aircraft, navy carrier-based aircraft, army antiaircraft artillery, civil airlines, civil defense, and a controller who would direct fighters once they were airborne. All of this was patterned after those proven systems used in the Battle of Britain and the newly established facilities on the East Coast.

The information center was the "filter center" that received warnings about approaching aircraft from the radar units. Once received, military personnel plotted these target's locations, and army or navy liaison officers made a determination on these target's intent. In that role, each of the aviation officers had to know about all of the anticipated flights of his particular branch. For example, an officer would be informed that the aircraft carrier *Lexington* would be approaching from 270 degrees on a given date, was some 100 miles away, and intended to launch its squadrons for arrival at Ford Island Naval Air Station. If none of the aviation interests could identify or claim an approaching aircraft, the planes were considered hostile, or "bogies." If the planes were determined to be hostile, the information center pursuit controller radioed an alert to fighters at Wheeler Field. They then flew toward the unidentified plots, and the U.S. fighter planes could be detected by radar and plotted at the center once airborne. While the pilots chased toward the target, the controller notified antiaircraft and searchlight units of the inbound bogies and sounded air raid sirens. While this complex process may seem arcane, the IFF (identification-friend-or-foe) transponder used in modern air traffic control was not available until mid-1942. [1]

The Army Signal Corps built the Hawaiian Aircraft Warning Service so that it could handle communications both by telephone and radio. General Short had directed the Signal Corps to construct the project and then work with the Hawaiian Air Force in getting it up and running. When the Signal Corps declared the project complete, some Signal Corps personnel and equipment were slated to transfer to the Air Force to help keep the center properly staffed. This transition, or its failure to be implemented on a timely basis, was one of the fatal flaws that preceded the climactic events of 7 December 1941. The Signal Corps guarded its turf jealously and was in no hurry to allow its radar operators and other technicians to be transferred to the junior Air Force branch. When the Aircraft Warning Service was completed and operational, Brigadier General Howard C. Davidson, head of the 14th Pursuit Wing, was placed in command. But during its construction and assembly phase, the Aircraft Warning Service was under control of Lieutenant Colonel Carroll A. Powell, the army's Hawaiian Department signal officer.

Meanwhile, Major Lorry N. Tindal, formerly commanding the 15th Pursuit Group at Wheeler Field, was charged with construction of what Davidson had labeled "the air defense project." An officer with considerable experience, Tindal was temporarily assigned to the Air Defense Command School in New York to study the fledgling efforts to develop an Aircraft Warning Service. He was uniquely qualified for the new high-tech apparatus. Before joining the Aircorps, he graduated from Clemson in 1928 with a degree in electrical engineering. On his return to Oahu, he began to assemble the basic elements of an information center in the attic of the 14th Pursuit Wing headquarters at Wheeler Field. In post-attack testimony, Tindal said that the effort involved ". . . what we could beg, borrow, or steal." [2]

When the information center was later established at Fort Shafter, Tindal was the initial fighter controller at the facility. Junior officers charged with conducting the day-to-day tasks of planning, supplying, and constructing the Aircraft Warning Service were then-Captain Kenneth P. Bergquist of the Air Corps and Captain Wilfred W. Tetley of the Signal Corps. Bergquist and Tetley, both West Pointers, had a mutual interest in getting their project up and running. Bergquist, a fighter pilot who had just commanded the 44th Pursuit Squadron, had a flair for administrative detail. He had attended the Mitchel Field Air Defense School with Tindal and was a qualified controller. Tetley was a former cavalryman who had transferred to the Signal Corps. He had an abiding interest in radio and commanded the Signal Corps Aircraft Warning Company. They worked together amicably, dividing the chores according to their special interests and expertise. But both were dogged by official foot dragging and the ambivalence of the other service branches. Ken Bergquist related one such incident:

> I sent in a requisition for aircraft headsets for members of the center. The Quartermaster Corps wanted to argue about why the Air Force was requisitioning equipment when the Signal Corps was supposed to be doing the job. I had to act. The Signal Corps people had no appreciation of the detect, account, and intercept process.

Nor did the rest of the army or most of the navy have much awareness of the newfangled radar, its potential, and how it had to be supplemented by plotting, identification, and fighter direction. Secrecy surrounding the radar units added to the general lack of understanding among army and navy officers. Lorry Tindal said: [There was] "a lack of push, a lack of interest, and a realization of what the thing [AWS] could do. It was sort of a toy and the services had to be sold on it." [3]

By mid-1941 the navy had installed CXAM search radar (similar to the SCR-270B) on the Pacific Fleet aircraft carriers *Lexington* and *Enterprise*, the battleship *California*, and the cruisers *Chicago*, *Chester*, and *Pensacola*. Their crews trained hard, learned the process of detection, plotted attackers, and—in the case of the carriers—controlled navy fighters for interception. At this vital juncture, a man imminently qualified in the subject of air defense appeared on the Hawaiian scene: Lieutenant Commander William E.G. "Bill" Taylor.

He had an impressive résumé that was unique in the navy. After studying aeronautical engineering at New York University, the navy recruited Taylor for flight training and he won his wings and a commission in the naval reserve in 1927. He served briefly as a pilot in Fighting Squadron 5 on the *Lexington*, but due to personnel limits was released from active duty and returned to reserve status after one year. In 1928 when the opportunity presented itself, he transferred to the Marine Corps Reserve, becoming a second lieutenant and a flight instructor.

In 1934, with all military services suffering the budgetary restraints of the Great Depression, he was again ordered to inactive status. Taylor piloted for United Airlines for several years, but with war clouds gathering in Europe, he volunteered his services to the British, and in September 1939 was commissioned a sub-lieutenant in the Fleet Air Arm. Flying Gloster Gladiators, he served with 804 Squadron on the carriers *Glorious* and *Furious* during the Norwegian Campaign and then performed intercept missions from Scapa Flow. After transferring to the Royal Air Force (RAF), he flew Hawker Hurricanes with 242 Squadron in 1940 in the defense of southern England. At this juncture, a number of Americans had joined the RAF and were training to fly as a unit in 71 Squadron. Taylor became their commander during the training phase. As the "Eagles" entered combat in 1941, the RAF decided that Taylor was too old for fighter operations, relieved him of the Eagle Squadron assignment, and offered him the rank of wing commander with an operational training unit. Bitterly disappointed at the loss of his command, he wanted to return to the U.S. Navy. The British obliged, and Taylor headed for Washington, D.C.

A handful of navy department officers recognized his breadth of experience, exceptional in the U.S. Navy at that time, and reinstated his reserve commission. He began a series of lectures to Atlantic Fleet aviation squadrons on the procedures for radar-controlled detection of raiders and radar-directed interception by carrier fighters. Then he was sent to the West Coast and Hawaii for radar consulting stints on Pacific Fleet carriers and lectures to active squadrons.

Captain Bergquist was visiting aboard the aircraft carrier *Enterprise*, attempting to further educate himself on the use of radar to locate enemy aircraft and control interceptors, when he met Taylor and realized his potential value to the air defense project. On Bergquist's suggestion, the army sought Taylor's services, and in October 1941 Admiral Kimmel made him a consultant of sorts.

Thus Taylor teamed up with Tindal, Bergquist, and Tetley, all of whom greeted him with great enthusiasm. Here was a man who had actually flown in combat and had been directed by a ground controller who could visualize the approach of enemy aircraft on a plotting board.

Working against a blend of ignorance and indifference, Davidson's junior officers soldiered on through the later half of 1941, managing to assemble and link the components of the Aircraft Warning Service system. What they could not produce was intra- and inter-service cooperation and assemble the essential around-the-clock staff. A letter to Admiral Kimmel, drafted by Colonel Powell and signed by General Short, contained the formal request of the army's Hawaiian Department for navy liaison officers. The 5 August 1941 communication said:

> The army's aircraft warning facilities for the Hawaiian Department are rapidly approaching completion. Small-scale operation is expected in the immediate future. Subsequent to the original setup the Aircraft Warning Service has been greatly augmented. The results of this augmentation, however, are not expected to materialize for some months.
>
> The Department Aircraft Warning Service Board, consisting of officers from all the instrumentalities associated with the air defense, has been reactivated and is now constituted as a liaison advisory council on AWS affairs. Inasmuch as the navy has shown considerable interest in the AWS and has initiated plans for a similar system of its own [search radar aboard ships], it seems greatly to the interest of both services to have a naval officer as contact or liaison officer between army and navy AWS activities. I believe that in this manner our efforts along these lines will be highly cumulative and that the prospects for future joint army-navy cooperation greatly enhanced.
>
> Accordingly, your assistance would be appreciated in effecting arrangements whereby an officer from your headquarters be detailed to serve as liaison officer between your headquarters and mine.

Admirals Kimmel and Bloch responded promptly, designating Commander Maurice E. Curts and Lieutenant C. B. Arney. [4]

The tone of the correspondence compels the assumption that none of the principals considered the liaison officers anything more than participants at infrequent planning or board meetings. Wilfred Tetley, deeply involved in creating the Aircraft Warning Service, doubts that Powell himself fully understood the mechanics of the information center and the need for round-the-clock watch officers, and the ambiguity of the Short letter would tend to support that.

In post-Pearl Harbor testimony, Kimmel and Bloch used this action and the later assignment of Lieutenant Commander Bill Taylor to excuse themselves from any charge that they did not cooperate in furnishing liaison watch officers to the information center. The senior Hawaiian officers were guilty of careless neglect with regard to their understanding of the Aircraft Warning Service and the need to staff the information center, one of the major command failures that led to the disaster of Pearl Harbor.

1. Roberts Commission, Part 22, pp. 119-120. Brigadier General Davidson attempts to explain the AWS process to the Roberts Panel.
2. Army Pearl Harbor Board, Part 29, p. 2291.
3. Ibid., p. 2295.
4. Letter from the commander in chief of the Pacific Navy dated 10 August 1941 to CG Hawaiian Department and 14th Naval District letter dated 9 August 1941 to CG Hawaiian Department.

Chapter 5

Looking Over the Horizon

The Aircraft Warning Service (AWS) was but one leg of the planned defense against an enemy attack of Oahu. The second and third legs were long-range reconnaissance, needed to give warning of the approach of enemy naval forces and the Hawaiian Bomber Command, with a standby heavy bomber fleet, would then try to strike that raiding force. Both distant-search capabilities and the attack group would come under navy command in the event of imminent hostilities.

While the Hawaiian Air Force had sought long-range bomber aircraft, it was consistently denied more than a token multi-engine bomber force because not enough heavy bombers—B-17 Flying Fortresses and B-24 Liberators—had been produced to cover U.S. military obligations over the entire globe. General Martin's single-engine fighters were of extremely limited range and were not permitted to fly out of sight of the Hawaiian Islands; hence they were useless for anything other than "in-shore" reconnaissance, meaning within sight of land. His bomber command was made up primarily of a force of 33 Douglas B-18 twin-engine aircraft belonging to the under-strength 5th and 11th bombardment groups.

The five-year-old B-18 had a modest bomb load, a top speed of just 217 miles per hour, and a feeble defense of three .30-caliber machine guns. By 1941 standards, it was inadequate for combat. Still, the Royal Canadian Air Force had outfitted 20 for anti-submarine work over the Atlantic, and by early 1941, the Army Air Force deployed squadrons of B-18s to the Canal Zone, the Caribbean, and Newfoundland for the long-range mission of sub hunting. [1]

General Martin disliked the B-18 as a bomber because of its lack of speed, poor defensive armament, and short operating radius (300 miles) with a bomb load, as he later testified. [2] Consequently, none of the 18th Bomb Wing's B-18s were armed or prepared for a strike mission, although the crews trained with bombs during mock exercises. The arming of the B-18s to repel a Japanese carrier force was to occur theoretically when the Joint Coastal Frontier Defense Plan was called into play.

Martin also had a handful of long-range, four-engine Boeing B-17D Flying Fortresses. Newer B-17Es periodically reaching Hawaii were transients, and the Hawaiian Air Force was charged with the role of training crews to ferry the Fortresses along an island-hopping route—Midway, Wake, Port Moresby, Darwin—to the Philippine air force on Luzon. There, the Forts were thought to constitute a sobering strategic threat to Formosa and Japanese naval forces that might operate in Southeast Asian waters. The B-17E, with better armament, larger bomb load, and an operating range of 800 miles, was the zenith of U.S. bomber development in 1941. Denied the 180 B-17s he sought for his search and attack needs and disdainful of making do with his aging B-18s, Martin had no effective long-range force capable of either reconnaissance or attack when the Japanese struck.

By December 1941, the Hawaiian Air Force counted only 12 B-17Ds in its inventory. Of these, six were out of commission for maintenance, as were 12 of the 33 B-18s. Thus, the Hawaiian Bomber Command concentrated on its training role and passing new B-17s along to Luzon. [3] In the absence of sufficient Hawaiian Bomber Command aircraft to perform reconnaissance, Oahu relied on the navy for all distant search. [4]

The navy's shore-based patrol aircraft was the Consolidated PBY Catalina, a twin-engine flying boat, slow and vulnerable to fighter attack, but possessing a maximum range of 1,300 miles. Bellinger was supplied with additional late-version PBY-5s as 1941 progressed but only had a total inventory (at Midway and Oahu) of 81 Catalinas by December 1941. He considered this number too few for distant reconnaissance on anything more than a random basis. [5]

The primary mission of the patrol squadrons was scouting ahead of the fleet and providing security against submarine attack in Oahu's approaches. On 5 December 1941, Patrol Squadron 22 had just returned to Oahu from duty at Midway and Wake, and its crews were in need of rest and aircraft in need of maintenance. On the eve of the Pearl Harbor attack, Patrol Squadron 21, with a dozen PBY-3s, was operating from Midway and supporting the carrier delivery of Marine aircraft. The rest of the navy patrol aircraft were at Oahu's Ford Island and Kaneohe Naval Air Station on Oahu's east coast. [6]

Bellinger and Martin estimated that 18 aircraft on a theoretical search, five degrees apart and to a distance of 700 miles, could effectively observe 144 degrees of the compass. It would take virtually all of the Oahu-based Catalinas for a 360-degree search. Bellinger felt that if he was to perform his primary assignment, to patrol ahead of the fleet, he could not be exhausting his force of Catalinas in other than hit-and-miss searches over 360 degrees. Hence, patrol wing assignments in the first week of December 1941 directed training and short-range sweeps of the fleet operating areas, including searches to the northwest, then a reduced schedule Friday through Sunday for routine repair and maintenance so as not to "deprecate the readiness" of the patrol wings, according to Lieutenant Commander Logan Ramsey. [7]

On the morning of 7 December 1941, seven of Bellinger's PBYs were aloft from Midway, patrolling to the east toward the Hawaiian Islands. The *Lexington* task force was approaching Midway from that sector. From Ford Island and Kaneohe, four PBYs were operating near Lahina Roads on a training exercise with U.S. submarines, and three more were patrolling the fleet operating areas near the approaches to Pearl Harbor. Several others were on standby status, but none were conducting distant reconnaissance from Oahu. Had Bellinger wished to do so, he had another 54 operable patrol planes left to perform distant search, including the recently returned VP-22. [8]

Without long-range Navy PBY or army bomber-reconnaissance aircraft aloft, the only possible warning of a Japanese strike force approaching Hawaii on 7 December 1941 would have to come from the several Aircraft Warning Service radar sets then operating on Oahu.

1. Wesley F. Craven and James L. Cate, *The Army Air Forces in World War II*, Volume I, p. 162.

2. Army Pearl Harbor Board, Part 28, p. 979.

3. Roberts Commission, Part 24, Exhibit T, p. 1833.

4. Joint Congressional Committee, Part 1, p. 378.

5. Roberts Commission, Part 22, p. 557.

6. Ibid., pp. 558-559.

7. Navy Court of Inquiry, Part 32, p. 446.

8. Roberts Commission, Part 22, pp. 556–584.

Chapter 6

Alerts, Drills, and Random Omens

Political tension between the United States and Japan reached an early peak in 1940 when President Roosevelt ordered the Pacific Fleet from its West Coast base to an indeterminate stay at Pearl Harbor. After that, successive diplomatic maneuvers between Japan and the Soviet Union sent Washington into a frenzy. As a consequence, the Hawaiian army command was ordered on what would be the first of many alerts on 17 June 1940:

> Immediately alert complete defensive organization to deal with transpacific raid to greatest extent possible without creating public hysteria or projecting undue curiosity of newspapers or alien agents. Suggest maneuver basis. Maintain alert until further orders. Instructions for secret communication direct with chief of staff will be furnished you shortly. [1]

On 24 June 1940, Major General Herron, Short's predecessor as head of the army's Hawaiian Department, wrote grandly of the performance of his charges during the month-long alert in a radiogram to the chief of staff:

> I have just come in from seeing the dawn patrols take the air and the antiaircraft standing to their guns at dawn. . . . I have been gratified by the precision with which the planes get off each morning at 4:30 A.M. [2]

Six months later, an event in Europe sent ripples toward the Pacific. On 11 November 1940, 21 British Swordfish torpedo bombers flying off the aircraft carrier *Illustrious* attacked the Italian fleet at anchor in the harbor of Taranto. The obsolete, biplane bombers sank or heavily damaged three battleships in the night attack, effectively eliminating the Italian navy as a meaningful force in the Mediterranean Sea. Every senior officer in the U.S. Navy was aware of the incident, and the Hawaiian command pondered the possibility of a duplication of this disaster in Pearl Harbor. The navy's Bureau of Ordnance assured them that because of Pearl's shallow depth, such a torpedo attack could not be successful. [3] But the implications of Taranto were not lost on the Japanese, who dispatched naval officers from their German diplomatic delegation to Italy for a firsthand study of the scene.

Admiral Kimmel had barely settled into his new job as fleet commander in chief when an eerie warning surfaced in Tokyo. On 27 January 1941, the U.S. ambassador to Japan, Joseph Grew, sent a coded message to Washington:

> A member of the embassy was told by my Peruvian colleague that from many quarters, including a

Japanese one, he had heard that a surprise attack on Pearl Harbor was planned by the Japanese military forces, in case of "trouble" between Japan and the United States; that the attack would involve the use of all the Japanese military forces. My colleague said that he was prompted to pass this on because it had come to him from many sources, although the plan seemed fantastic. [4]

The chief of naval operations passed the message along to Admiral Kimmel with an endorsement from navy intelligence saying, in effect, that he likewise considered it fantastic. But it would be the first of many 1941 incidents that detailed the possibility of the United States being attacked.

General Short had just assumed his new command when he received a February warning from Secretary of War Stimson. It said in part: ". . . If war eventuates with Japan, it is believed easily possible that hostilities would be initiated by a surprise attack upon the fleet or naval base at Pearl Harbor." [5]

Among the periodic messages Admiral Stark sent to Kimmel was this one dated 1 April 1941 that said the following:

Personnel of your naval intelligence service should be advised that because of the fact that past experience shows the Axis powers often begin activities in a particular field on Saturdays and Sundays or on national holidays of the country concerned, they should take steps on such days to see that proper watches and precautions are in effect. [6]

By July 1941, as frustrations grew over the continued Japanese aggression, President Roosevelt initiated stronger measures, and the United States began imposing further economic sanctions that created a virtual cessation of trade. This prompted a joint message from the army and navy to the respective Hawaiian commanders warning them of the worsening situation. It was ominous, but short of a full-scale alert:

> Chief of naval operations and chief of staff, do not anticipate immediate hostile reaction by Japanese through the use of military means, but you are furnished this information in order that you may take appropriate precautionary measures against any possible eventualities. Action is being initiated by the United States Army to call the Philippine army into active service at an early date. Except from immediate army subordinates, the contents of this dispatch are to be kept secret. [7]

The gravity of the international situation and the ever-present realization that the vast majority of the Oahu population was of Japanese descent caused the term "borderline war-time status" to make its appearance in military communications. Protective bunkers for the aircraft of the 14th Pursuit Wing were nearly completed at Wheeler Field, but scattering the planes about the perimeter of the airdrome presented a different security problem. Wheeler was not fenced, and a public road ran through its eastern border. Fighters and alert crews could be made safer from air attack in the bunkers but were more exposed to possible sabotage, which the army assumed would occur in a war with Japan. Scattering men and aircraft to the bunkers also created a manpower problem for the 14th Pursuit

Wing. The unit's crews not only had to service aircraft at a distance from hangars, fuel, ammunition, and parts storage, but the same crews were expected to guard the planes day and night. Hickam Field had a similar perimeter problem.

General Short, ever the infantryman, seemed oblivious to the double-duty of the aviation ground crews. In fact, Short looked on his 7,000 Air Force enlisted personnel as an untapped source of ground troops. He issued an order to train aviation mechanics as infantrymen who could guard Schofield Barracks when the infantry regiments marched to quell an internal uprising or confront an invasion. He ordered a force of 1,500 airmen to be brought into an emergency reserve, despite the fact that he had two infantry divisions, the 24th and 25th, more than 10,000 troops, plus support units. These troops had some assignments to defend beaches and guard key installations in the event of an invasion.

But with the absence of a war alert, most of them sat in their barracks just off the northern boundary of Wheeler Field. Generals Martin and Davidson protested the order to Short and also to Air Force headquarters in Washington. [8] This wasteful practice of using highly trained aviation technicians from the air defense system as supplemental infantry continued even after the attack on 7 December 1941, until Short was relieved of command.

The intermittent warnings of impending hostilities began to be coupled with systematic air raid drills. From April 1941 through November, 13 simulated war games in and around Oahu were conducted, with navy aircraft frequently acting as aggressors and the Hawaiian Air Force defending (see Appendix B). Both army and navy shore-based aircraft operated along with antiaircraft batteries. Air raid sirens provided a sense of realism to Oahu residents. Captains Bergquist and Tetley ran additional informal exercises on their own initiative to train Aircraft Warning Service crews and test the system.

The May 1941 games involved a simulated attack on approaching navy carrier forces and the repelling of a mock amphibious invasion. Short enthusiastically wrote to General Marshall about how his B-17s had found the enemy force at a distance of 250 miles and described how his infantry units had repelled the landing. The search and high-altitude bombing were mock exercises, and the invasion was an unlikely scenario. But the infantryman in Short preferred practicing the ground games over practicing for the most probable event, a surprise air raid. [9]

The last of the SCR-270B mobile radar sets, long sought by the Hawaiian command, finally arrived dockside on 4 August 1941. A week later, the last site selections were approved. When the first two of the radar units were operational, Aircraft Warning Service officers felt that their temporary information center at Fort Shafter was ready for a dress rehearsal.

On 27 September 1941—a full 10 weeks before the Pearl Harbor attack—a drill was held involving all elements of the military. The Aircraft Warning Service personnel were pleased with the results, as illustrated by a letter from Lieutenant Colonel Carroll Powell, Hawaiian Department signal officer, to the chief of the army materiel branch:

> This exercise was started approximately 4:30 in the morning and with three radio [radar] sets in operation. We noted when the planes took off from the airplane carriers in the oscilloscope. We determined this distance to be approximately 80 miles, due to the fact that the planes would circle around waiting the assemblage of the remainder from the carrier. As soon as the planes were assembled, they proceeded towards Hawaii. This was very easily determined, and within six minutes the pursuit aircraft

were notified and they took off and intercepted the incoming bombers at approximately 30 miles from Pearl Harbor.

It was a very interesting exercise. All the general officers present were highly pleased with the proceedings of the radio direction finding sets [Powell is still referring to the radar] and the personnel associated with the information centers.

We have had very little trouble with the operations of these sets. When the fixed stations are installed in the higher mountains surrounding Hawaii, we expect to have as good an air warning system available for use as is now operating for the British on their tight little island, as their situation is approximately the same as ours is on Hawaii. [10]

The recollection of Second Lieutenant Grover White, part of the Signal Corps team at the information center, reflected a slightly different view of the test results:

When the "attack" didn't take place on schedule, some of them [senior observers] were getting a little bit antsy at having to get up so early. Then the plots began appearing, and interest picked up, particularly when the line of plots from Oahu [the army interceptors] headed straight for the line of arrows headed for Oahu [the navy attackers]. When the two lines met, I'll bet they heard Ken Bergquist holler "Geronimo" all the way to Wheeler and Schofield.

Despite the success of the 27 September drill in detecting the approach of the *Enterprise* air group from 224 degrees, with a range of 84 miles, and the ability of the information center to direct alert army interceptors against them, nothing changed in the lethargic approach of the Hawaiian command structure toward the subject of air defense. The worker bees in the Aircraft Warning Service continued adding to and improving their system and practiced drills well into November. But they proceeded without the momentum needed from General Short to activate the entire system. In fact, Short was so ignorant to the evolution of the Aircraft Warning Service and the watershed test of 27 September 1941 that he later testified to the Roberts Commission that it was his recollection that the radar had not been available before 1 November 1941. He, of course, was wrong. [11]

In addition to his work at the Fort Shafter Information Center, Lieutenant Commander Bill Taylor pursued the navy hierarchy and tried to coax its cooperation. In addition to more watch officers, the AWS wanted navy antiaircraft guns that were on ships in port to be controlled by the center along with army batteries. The plan was that the information center, when suitably manned, could distinguish friendly aircraft from bogies. Admiral Bloch refused Taylor's request, saying that "no army organization would control guns on any navy vessel. If anything comes over, we will shoot it down." [12] Indeed this proved sadly true, as on 7 December 1941 navy ships' batteries downed friend and foe alike who approached Pearl Harbor, including several aircraft from the *Enterprise* air group. [13]

Although the navy respected Lieutenant Commander Taylor for his experience and knowledge of radar and intercept control, he nonetheless labored in vain to establish the needed teams of navy liaison officers. Staffing at the information center required two teams per day from the carrier community and from shore-based navy-marine units for daylight eight-hour shifts. Night operation would require a third team. Kimmel's office told Taylor that 14th Naval District, Bloch's command, would supply liaison officers. Taylor received no cooperation from Bloch and was shunted to Bellinger, who said he had no one to spare from the patrol wings. Returning to Kimmel's office on 1 December, Taylor reported his failure; he had touched base with every senior member of Kimmel's staff in his quest, yet he had been met with complete indifference. "During the entire period of my duty at the information center, I made frequent visits to CINCPAC's office and conferred with his chief of staff [Smith], operations officer [DeLany], air officer [Davis] or communications officer [Curts]." [14]

The final word from the navy was that it would supply liaison officers when war was declared. The Joint Coastal Frontier Defense Plan emphasized that eventually either a formal declaration of war or an order from the president to mobilize (M-Day) would occur. However, the plan also noted that the likeliest form of initial enemy action would be a surprise air strike. In the interim, the navy told Taylor that if the Aircraft Warning Service personnel would phone navy officials, they would make every attempt to cooperate in identifying radar plots as hostile or friendly. No one in the navy, except Taylor, seemed able to appreciate the need for instant accounting of radar contacts at the information center in order to scramble interceptors and alert antiaircraft defenses in a timely fashion.

The Army Air Forces were not without their own liaison personnel problems. Brigadier General Jacob Rudolph advised Ken Bergquist that his 18th Bomb Wing was too busy training air crews for transpacific ferry service to spare liaison watch officers for the Aircraft Warning Service information center. [15]

General Davidson departed for the mainland with Colonel Powell to inspect a new air defense system being established in Seattle, while

Ken Bergquist (promoted to major) began instructing the pursuit squadrons in the process of detection, accounting, and interception. Bergquist also pushed completion of the telephone lines direct to the various squadrons. Communication from the information center still went to the Wheeler switchboard. With this exception, all information center phone lines were in place.

Through November, Admiral Stark had sent a flurry of secret messages to Kimmel regarding curious Japanese merchant ship activity and the routing of critical U.S. shipping. On 24 November 1941, Kimmel received a warning from Admiral Stark that gave the Pacific Fleet commander an ominous heads up. It read:

> Chances of favorable outcome of negotiations with Japan very doubtful. This situation, coupled with statements of Japanese government and movements of their naval and military forces, indicate in our opinion that a surprise aggressive movement in any direction including attack on the Philippines or Guam is a possibility. Chief of staff has seen this dispatch concurs and requests action to inform senior army officers in their areas. Utmost secrecy necessary in order not to complicate an already tense situation or precipitate Japanese action. Guam will be informed separately. [16]

On this same date, the air defense of Oahu took another gradual step toward completion with a meeting of the joint Aircraft Warning Service steering committee. The gathering included Lieutenant Colonel W. H. Murphy, acting Hawaiian Department signal officer; Lieutenant Commander Charles Coe, Patrol Wing 2; Major Tindal, 18th Bomb Wing; Lieutenant Commander Taylor, U.S. Navy personnel on detained service to the AWS; Major Bergquist, 14th Pursuit Wing; Lieutenant Grover White, Signal Corps Air Warning Service; Lieutenant Harville, 53rd Coast Artillery; Lieutenant Jay P. Thomas, 86th Observation Squadron; and Captain Tetley of the AWS, serving as recorder. The consensus of the committee was that the information center should become operational "on a full-time basis (0600 to 1800) as early as possible."

The minutes of this meeting—13 days before the attack—specifically make reference to the problem that Lieutenant Commander Coe, supposedly a navy liaison officer who was only attending steering committee meetings, might be withdrawn at any time because Patrol Wing 2 was not a permanently based shore unit. The minutes suggested " ... that the Commandant of the 14th Naval District [Bloch] be approached with a view to obtaining naval liaison officers and coordinating the information for all naval activities, ashore and afloat." [17] Taylor tried again to cajole the navy into cooperating, but nothing came of the effort.

The last three SCR-270B radar units finally were placed at their intended sites and linked with the information center on 26 November 1941. The Aircraft Warning Service then had six mobile radars in hand on Oahu.

With growing annoyance, the war department, which had been pushing for the Aircraft Warning Service to be formalized, issued a directive to that end on 15 September 1941. In a letter of 25 September 1941, General Martin responded to General Arnold that he hoped to have the new Fort Shafter Information Center in operation within 30 days. [18]

The army's Hawaiian Department finally established an air defense board (replacing the old air defense planning board) on 2 December. Davidson was designated chairman; Bergquist, recorder; and the other six appointees were from the Signal Corps, Coast

Artillery, and Air Force. The board was unable to gather all parties for a meeting prior to the attack. [19]

The army fighters, for their part, were cocked and primed; they were the ones standing alerts in the bunkers about Wheeler Field. Ground crews virtually "lived" next to their assigned planes. Alert pilots, rotated by squadron, were dressed in flight suits and either sat in their cockpits or lounged in the under-wing shade. One of the young lieutenants, Tuevo E. "Gus" Ahola (later a colonel) recalled the drudgery of the continuous alerts:

> We were under virtual house arrest. It was tough to get your laundry done and get to the PX. We were in our flight suits for a week at a time and got pretty ripe. They had a rule at the officers' club that lunch would not be served to officers not in Class A uniform, but that had to be relaxed because of the seemingly endless alert situation.

The pursuit squadron commanders and most flight leaders were all seasoned pilots with near 1,000 hours of flight time. Many of the junior pilots were from the Flying Class of 1940D but still logged 500 to 600 hours, half of it in fighters. About a third of these newest pilots came to Hawaii after flight-school graduation that year. Those who survived through 1942 would become veteran combat leaders.

The frequency of the Hawaiian air raid drills and their realistic conduct was such that when they were undertaken, radio messages went to all shore and ship stations advising "Drill. Danger of air raid on Pearl Harbor exists. Drill" (see Appendix B).

Claire Chennault, formerly of the Army Air Corps and then chief of the Chinese air force, passed through Honolulu on a Pan American flight to Asia in July 1941 and conducted a virtual intelligence briefing on Pacific war prospects. Lieutenant Charlie Taylor (later colonel), another of the 1940D flyers, recalled the impact of the gathering:

> The meeting was held at the Wheeler Field officers' club and was packed. Chennault was a spellbinder who spoke for nearly three hours. He told us his experiences in China and reviewed the quality of Japanese flyers and their new fighter, the Mitsubishi Zero. He said that we would be surprised at its agility and sharp-turning characteristics.
>
> He discussed the volunteer force he was assembling [American Volunteer Group, popularly known as the Flying Tigers] and the financial benefits. He told us that we could resign our commissions and be reinstated in good standing at a later date, but he didn't press the solicitation.
>
> Chennault closed by saying that war between the United States and Japan was imminent—just a matter of months.
>
> A day or so after this gathering an order was issued freezing all Hawaiian pilots in their existing jobs. Somebody felt that we would be needed soon in our current assignments.

1. Roberts Commission, Part 24, Exhibit 34, p. 2147.
2. Ibid.
3. Joint Congressional Committee, Part 17, Exhibit 116, p. 2700.
4. Ibid., Part 21, Exhibit 15.
5. Ibid., Part 39, p. 233.
6. Ibid., Part 8, p. 3487.
7. Roberts Commission, Part 24, Exhibit 34.

8. Army Pearl Harbor Board, Part 28, p. 957 and pp. 981–987.

9. Joint Congressional Committee, Part 15, 1622-23.

10. Ibid., Part 18, Exhibit 136.

11. Roberts Commission, Part 22, p. 35.

12. Hart Inquiry, Part 26, p. 381.

13. Ibid., pp. 382–385.

14. Roberts Commission, Part 24, pp. 1393, 1394, and 1650.

15. Army Pearl Harbor Board, Part 27, p. 630.

16. Joint Congressional Committee, Part 14, Exhibit 37, pp. 1403–1405.

17. HQ, 14th Pursuit Wing, 26 November 1941, Subject: Minutes of Joint Aircraft Warning Service Steering Committee.

18. Army Pearl Harbor Board, Part 28, p. 981.

19. Letter of direction from headquarters, Hawaiian Department, 2 December 1941, Subject: Air Defense Organization.

Chapter 7

The Eve of Disaster

On 26 November 1941, Japan's First Air Fleet, commanded by Vice Admiral Chuichi Nagumo, departed southeast from Etorofu Island in the Kuriles into the northern Pacific. Bound for the Hawaiian Islands, Nagumo chose a route through the ocean expanse that avoided shipping lanes and ordered strict radio silence. The task force consisted of six aircraft carriers, two battleships, two heavy cruisers, one light cruiser, nine destroyers, and three submarines. A train of eight tankers and supply ships accompanied the fleet. An advance force of 20 additional fleet submarines was also deployed to the Hawaiian Islands. Five of them carried midget submarines that were given the mission of penetrating Pearl Harbor.

As the Japanese naval task force departed for a historic action that would tumble the United States into World War II and precipitate the destruction of the Japanese empire, the tocsins began to sound in Hawaii, day by day.

THURSDAY, 27 NOVEMBER 1941

Washington had no specific intelligence regarding the movement of the Japanese carrier strike force, but the deteriorating state of international affairs between the two nations caused a sense in the capital that war was looming. Accordingly, separate, secret messages were dispatched. Historic in their content, they were war warnings. The message from Marshall to Short read:

> Negotiations with Japanese appear to be terminated to all practical purposes, with only the barest possibilities that the Japanese government might come back and offer to continue. Japanese future action unpredictable, but hostile action possible at any moment. If hostilities cannot, repeat cannot, be avoided, the United States desires that Japan commit the first overt act. This policy should not, repeat not, be construed as restricting you to a course of action that might jeopardize your defense. Prior to hostile Japanese action, you are directed to undertake such reconnaissance and other measures as you deem necessary but these measures should be carried out so as not, repeat not, to alarm the civil population or disclose intent. Report measures taken. Should hostilities occur, you will carry out the tasks assigned in Rainbow 5 as far as they pertain to Japan. Limit dissemination of this highly secret information to minimum essential officers. [1]

This was the message to General Short. A similar message was sent simultaneously to Kimmel by Admiral Stark. Kimmel's message opened with the sentence: "This despatch [sic] is to be considered a war warning" and contained additional intelligence regarding Japanese naval movements toward the Kra Peninsula in Southeast Asia.

Short's response seemed to demonstrate a crucial misreading of the message from Washington: "Report department alerted to sabotage. Liaison with navy. Short." [2] This confused reply went unchallenged and unanswered, a monumental oversight by General Marshall.

As the extraordinary "war warning" arrived, the two Hawaiian military chiefs were considering the reinforcement of garrisons on Wake and Midway islands, an action that had been prompted by earlier messages of 16 October and 24 November from Washington.

Short offered two newly organized squadrons of fighters—the 72nd and 73rd Pursuit—each equipped with a dozen Curtiss P-40s. He proposed sending them, along with infantry units, to garrison the island bases. In exchange, he demanded control of the islands then considered navy property. Kimmel declined the offer, explaining (correctly) that once the squadrons of short-range, land-based fighters had been launched to the islands from carriers, the P-40s would be stranded. Army fighters had flown off aircraft carriers, but they were not equipped for a carrier landing.

The results of this joint command session were that the navy undertook the reinforcement of the two remote outposts with the Marine Fighting Squadron VMF-211 and Marine Scout Bombing Squadron VMSB-231, plus additional Marine troops for the Wake Island defense battalion. These units departed aboard the *Enterprise* (28 November) and *Lexington* (5 December), respectively, each supported by cruisers and destroyers. Vice Admiral William F. Halsey, commanding Task Force 8 in *Enterprise*, with Wake reinforcements, met with Admiral Kimmel before his departure, saw the war warning dispatch, and was cautioned that the situation with Japan was critical. Kimmel told him, "Use your common sense." From his own assessment, Halsey believed that war was imminent and that they would be fighting before his return to Pearl Harbor. So he proceeded cautiously with his ships on a zigzag course, scouting aircraft aloft, and placed a combat air patrol over the task force during daylight hours. As Task Force 8 approached Wake, Halsey ordered a higher state of readiness. [3]

Rear Admiral John H. Newton, commanding Task Force 12 with the *Lexington* bound for Midway, was not asked to confer with Kimmel and had no advice regarding the recent navy department warnings. He was not even notified regarding the mission or location of Halsey's task force. However, based on his own interpretation of the situation, he believed that he might be going in harm's way. He followed a zigzag course and had *Lexington* aircraft scouting in advance of his task force. [4]

Because of the island reinforcement mission, these two task forces were spared the Japanese attack on 7 December 1941. The *Lexington* and her escorts were 425 miles southeast of Midway and aborted their mission when advised of the attack on Pearl Harbor. The *Enterprise* and her consorts were 150 miles west of Oahu. She would be delayed in reaching Pearl Harbor on 6 December because of rough seas. The Pacific Fleet's third aircraft carrier, the *Saratoga,* left San Diego on the morning of 8 December bound for Pearl Harbor. In addition to her own brood of 80-odd aircraft, she carried 14 F2A-3 Brewster Buffalo fighters of Marine Fighting Squadron VMF-221.

Officials in Washington ordered the Wake-Midway reinforcement, but for some reason, the tow top Hawaiian commanders did not see a similar need to ratchet up their defenses in nearby Oahu.

FRIDAY, 28 NOVEMBER 1941

Over the next few days, each command received further warning advisories from their respective senior officials in Washington. None were identical, but all were ambiguous or limited in their amplification of what those in Washington knew. Short and Kimmel reviewed their 27 November war warnings in face-to-face meetings, then each set about on a different degree of readiness, never again exchanging whatever intelligence the subsequent warnings provided. General Short terminated the existing No. 2 alert (against air attack) and went into the army's Alert No. 1, a full defense against sabotage. Thus, Short diverted his attention from the historic foe, a Japanese carrier strike, to a concern over internal disorder.

One immediate effect of this move was that General Martin was ordered to pull his fighter aircraft out of their protective air raid bunkers and assemble them on the apron at Wheeler in front of the hangars, where they could be more easily guarded from saboteurs. Colonel Bill Flood, commanding Wheeler Field, protested the order that his fighters be moved from protective bunkers. Martin told him those were Short's orders. Martin added that dispersal might alarm the population. [5]

However, the fighters had been occupying the U-shaped earthen bunkers for some weeks without alarming the populace, and the war warning had referred to hostile action. The war warning also had stated that defenses were not to be jeopardized and had directed reconnaissance, all implying an attack by conventional forces from outside Oahu.

Personnel of the fighter squadrons breathed a sigh of relief at the stand-down ordered by Short. The incessant campouts ended on 28 November, and exhausted Army Air Force enlisted personnel, who had been performing double duty, were back to a more normal peacetime status. But pilots were restricted to the base until Saturday, 6 December.

Short also personally directed that the new radar stations should operate from 4 to 7 A.M., the "danger hours," as he appropriately characterized them, and he directed that the Aircraft Warning

Service information center be manned "for training" during those same hours. But he did nothing about the recalcitrance of other military organizations that neglected to provide liaison officers to the center and posed no requirement that the 14th Pursuit Wing be placed on standby. Alert No. 1 called for a four-hour readiness notice for fighter aircraft, but the range of the radar units—150 miles maximum—would only provide a one-hour advance warning if bogies were detected. [6]

Aircraft Warning Service insiders were perplexed and dismayed. Major Bergquist asked Lieutenant Colonel W. H. Murphy, acting as Hawaiian Department signal officer in Powell's absence, "What the hell are you going to do with the information? If you get some radar plots, how are you going to identify them? And if no fighters are on alert status, who is going to react?"

"Those are the orders," was Murphy's response, obviously referring to Short's orders.

Bergquist did what he could. He prepared a schedule assigning information center watch officers from among senior pursuit pilots (excluding squadron commanders) to man the center from 4 A.M. to 4 P.M., from 2 through 11 December. He exceeded Short's rather limited 4 to 7 A.M. requirement because he wanted to get as many fighter pilots as possible familiar with the Aircraft Warning Service system. There was a specified post at the information center for a pursuit officer. If Bergquist was incapable of compelling the cooperation of 18th Bomb Wing or the navy to provide liaison officers, he at least had the rank and authority to fill the pursuit post.

SATURDAY, 29 NOVEMBER 1941

Honolulu Star-Bulletin headline: "U.S. Awaits Japan Reply." Excerpt: "Secretary of State Cordell Hull and Viscount Halifax, British ambassador, conferred today for an hour over the critical oriental situation and waited to see whether Japan will choose war or peace in the Pacific."

SUNDAY, 30 NOVEMBER 1941

Honolulu Advertiser headlines: "Japanese May Strike over Weekend" and "Kurusu Bluntly Warned Nation Ready for Battle."

The newspapers had no special intelligence sources, but merely speculated on Japanese intentions. They came closer to reality than either of Hawaii's top commanders with all their intelligence sources and warnings.

For many months leading up to the Pearl Harbor attack, officials in Washington consistently did not relay daily decrypts of Japanese diplomatic message traffic to senior military commanders in Hawaii. The reason offered by those in Washington after the attack was the need to protect the highly sensitive code-breaking process. However, Hawaiian commanders, as well as every officer and enlisted man, were kept informed of the diplomatic crisis by Honolulu newspapers despite being denied code-breaking secrets. Kimmel and Short could not have been sanguine in the face of international news coverage.

Personnel of the unique Signal Company Aircraft Warning Hawaii unit sensed the gathering war clouds. The commanding officer Captain Wilfred Tetley said:

Based on our assignment, we had an acute awareness, an undercurrent of anticipation that did not come down through the chain of command. Personnel of the company began a mess hall pool on when the Japanese attack would occur, probably on a Sunday or a holiday.

MONDAY, 1 DECEMBER 1941

Honolulu Advertiser headline: "Hull, Kurusu in Crucial Meeting." Excerpt: "Some unofficial quarters asserted that Japanese Premier General Hideki Tojo's speech on Saturday indicated that Japan may possibly have decided upon war."

Honolulu Star-Bulletin headline: "U.S. Army Alerted in Manila; Singapore Mobilizing as War Tension Grows; War Fear Grows in Philippines."

TUESDAY, 2 DECEMBER 1941

Honolulu Advertiser headline: "Japan Called Still Hopeful of Making Peace with U.S.; Japan Gives Two Weeks More to Negotiate." Excerpt from Japanese English-language newspaper Asahi: "We are deeply impressed that the negotiations are heading toward a finale without any hope of success."

Washington code breakers had been reading Japan's diplomatic wires for months, the code named "purple" and a process dubbed "magic." (Purple referred to the cover of the bindings in the Office of Naval Intelligence in which the diplomatic code data was kept, and Magic referred to the magicians who could read the Japanese codes.) It was so secret that only a handful of people in Washington knew of the breakthrough, and they limited dissemination of this knowledge so severely that neither Kimmel nor Short was aware of the process. Each of them relied mostly on a mix of spoon-fed intelligence from

Washington and the limited amount their own intelligence staffs could gather. Kimmel relied heavily on Lieutenant Commander Edwin T. Layton, a Pacific Fleet intelligence officer, and Lieutenant Commander Joseph J. Rochefort, Kimmel's chief cryptanalyst, for information on the whereabouts of the Japanese fleet. The latter headed a team at the 14th Naval District that monitored Japanese naval radio traffic. A meticulous analysis of that intercepted material permitted studied guesswork as to fleet movements and, to a lesser extent, intentions, although the Japanese had recently changed their naval codes.

Over the postwar years, those who are not specialists have disagreed about the U.S. efforts and successes in breaking the Japanese diplomatic code (Purple) and the Japanese navy operational code (JN-25). These were separate and carried very different information. The former was being read before the Pearl Harbor attack; the latter— to the extent that it yielded useful intelligence—only from the spring of 1942. Still many persons, among them historians, continue to confuse these issues.

When the Japanese Pearl Harbor strike force departed its Inland Sea bases in late November for a rendezvous in the Kurile Islands, a strict radio silence was imposed. In periodic intelligence briefings with Admiral Kimmel, Commander Edwin Layton presented him with a location sheet showing the estimated status of major Japanese navy warships. On 2 December, Layton had such a meeting with Kimmel and had noted the following about two Japanese carrier divisions: "Unknown—home waters."

Kimmel reacted with alarm:

> "Then you don't know where Carrier Division 1 and Carrier Division 2 are?"
>
> "No, sir, I do not," responded Layton. "I think they are in home waters, but I do not know for sure

where they are. But I feel pretty confident of the location of the rest of the units."

"Do you mean they could be rounding Diamond Head and you wouldn't know it?"

"I hope they would have been spotted before now," responded Layton. [7]

Regardless of his professed anxiety, Kimmel failed to share the worrisome information of the missing Japanese carrier divisions with Short. Nor did the mysterious absence of the carriers spur Kimmel to reconsider the employment of his PBY Catalina patrol planes, submarines, or surface ships in searching the appropriate approaches to Oahu, just in case.

WEDNESDAY, 3 DECEMBER 1941

Honolulu Advertiser headline: "Huge Pincer Attack on U.S. by Japan, France Predicted." Excerpt, a quote from Senator Claude Pepper: "Hitler, in effect, is attempting to give us war on two fronts."

Kimmel received another secret message from the chief of naval operations that should have ratcheted up the anxiety level:

Highly reliable information has been received that categoric [sic] and urgent instructions were sent yesterday to Japanese diplomatic and consular posts at Hong Kong, Singapore, Batavia, Manila, Washington, and London to destroy most of their codes and ciphers at once and to burn all other important and secret documents. [8]

Burning sensitive documents was a routine exercise in diplomatic and military housekeeping. But the destruction of codes was an unusual step that generally meant an escalation toward open hostilities.

Short did not receive a similar message, nor did Kimmel share this one with him. However, Short's own intelligence section became aware of document burning at the Japanese consulate in Honolulu. Dozens of Japanese intelligence agents posing as diplomats operated with diplomatic immunity from this center. Colonel Kendall J. Fielder, Short's intelligence officer, saw nothing of significance in the burning of papers as his office periodically did the same with sensitive material.

General Davidson and Lieutenant Colonel Powell returned from the mainland on board the passenger liner SS *Lurline* on 3 December. Davidson was puzzled at the change of orders by Short from No. 2 alert to the sabotage No. 1 alert, but he assumed that the commanding general must have had intelligence that he lacked.

THURSDAY, 4 DECEMBER 1941

Honolulu Star-Bulletin headline: "Japan Spurns U.S. Program."

FRIDAY, 5 DECEMBER 1941

Honolulu Advertiser headline: "Pacific Zero Hour Near; Japan Answers U.S. Today."

The Japanese ambassador Kichisaburo Nomura had been joined by special envoy Saburo Kurusu to conduct negotiations in Washington as the diplomatic situation reached its zenith. The top military commanders in Hawaii were not kept abreast of the detailed political developments except for what they could read in the newspapers. However, the news was sufficiently alarming that many members of military families were preparing to leave Hawaii.

The aircraft carrier *Lexington* and her escorting warships, Task Force 12, left Pearl Harbor for Midway in a condition of low readiness, but with ships zigzagging and scouting flights aloft.

In accordance with the joint defense agreement, the Hawaiian Air Force reported to Rear Admiral Bellinger that the following aircraft were available as a strike force against an aggressor fleet: 8 B-17s, 21 B-18s, and 6 A-20s. The B-18s were aircraft that General Martin later would declare unsuited for even a reconnaissance role because he considered them obsolete. [9]

SATURDAY, 6 DECEMBER 1941

> *Honolulu Advertiser* headlines: "America Expected to Reject Japan's Reply on Indochina; Japanese Navy Moving South." Excerpt: "Detailed recommendations for administration of the Hawaii Defense Act, otherwise known as the M-Day Law, were received by Governor Poindexter yesterday from his advisory council on civilian defense preparations."

> *Honolulu Star-Bulletin* headlines: "Singapore on War Footing," "New Peace Effort Urged in Tokyo," and "Civilians Urged to Leave Manila." [10]

At this date the undetected Japanese carrier strike force was some 640 miles northwest of Oahu and began moving toward its predetermined aircraft launching point, 220 miles due north of Oahu.

The *Lurline*, having turned around within 72 hours, sailed from Honolulu filled with service members' wives and children who were being returned to the mainland because of the rising tensions.

Among the passengers were Captain Wilfred Tetley, his wife, and his children. Tetley had orders assigning him to 14 days of temporary duty for Western Air Defense Command exercises with the 4th Interceptor Command, near San Francisco, which was part of his continuing education in air defense.

At Wheeler Field, 6 December was a normal, peacetime Saturday. That morning a review was held on the ramp with each squadron's aircraft aligned and dovetailed with those of the next squadron. Pilots, crew chiefs, and armorers stood by their individual aircraft, a Saturday formation ritual. When the troops were dismissed, ammunition was removed from aircraft and stored in Hangar No. 3 according to peacetime procedure, and all but essential officers were given the weekend off. This was all in keeping with orders passed down from General Short's headquarters for a stand-down.

First Lieutenant Lew Sanders, commanding the 46th Pursuit Squadron, was happy for the time off but was dismayed that no fighters were left on alert. From his reading of the news, he assumed that war was imminent.

Two pursuit squadrons were not at Wheeler. The 47th had been temporarily posted earlier in the week for gunnery practice to Haleiwa landing strip on the north coast. The 44th had been stationed at Bellows Field on the Oahu's east coast. Only one pilot officer remained at Haleiwa and just three were present at Bellows as their mates headed for Honolulu.

The only plane of the 14th Pursuit Wing aloft on Saturday afternoon was a Sikorsky OA-8 amphibian flown by the diligent Major Bergquist. He logged three hours while calibrating his radar units.

Navy warships moored in Pearl Harbor were on a similar stand-down, with many officers and seamen dismissed from shipboard duty for the weekend. Battleships moored on the east shore of Ford Island had not placed anti-torpedo nets, since the Navy Bureau of

Ordnance declared that a torpedo attack in Pearl Harbor's 40 to 45 feet of water could not succeed. Most warships had some antiaircraft guns ready for action, although in some ships the "ready" ammunition was padlocked.

During the afternoon of 6 December, the Federal Bureau of Investigation (FBI) translated a long-distance telephone call from a Honolulu dentist of Japanese descent, Dr. Motokazu Mori, to a person at the Tokyo newspaper *Yomiuri Shimbun*. The FBI regularly tapped some of the phone lines of suspect Japanese aliens and the many Japanese consular officials in Hawaii. In a disjointed discussion, sometimes inane, questions surfaced about aircraft, the Pacific Fleet, and searchlights. Thinking the implications were serious, the FBI contacted intelligence offices of both the navy and the army. The navy's Lieutenant Commander Irving H. Mayfield put off the matter until the next day. The army registered more concern. [11]

Lieutenant Colonel George W. Bicknell, the Hawaiian Department's assistant intelligence officer, thought the conversation was sufficiently suspicious to review with his superior, Colonel Kendall Fielder, who was scheduled to dine with General Short that evening. Both waited in Short's quarters until Bicknell could arrive with the Mori translation. Short and Fielder found nothing sinister in the rambling conversation between Mori and Tokyo, dismissed the matter, and went on to their planned dinner. [12]

1. Roberts Commission, Part 24, p. 2165.
2. Ibid.
3. Hart Inquiry, Part 26, pp. 322–324.
4. Ibid., p. 343.
5. Army Pearl Harbor Board, Part 28, pp. 1485–1494.
6. Roberts Commission, Part 22, p. 35.
7. Rear Admiral Edwin T. Layton with Roger Pineau and John Costello, *And I Was There*, pp. 243-244.
8. Hart Inquiry, Part 26, Exhibit 11, p. 489.
9. Hewitt Inquiry, Part 36, p. 289.
10. Joint Congressional Committee, Part 30, Exhibit 19, pp. 2974–2976.
11. Joint Congressional Committee, Part 15, Exhibit 84, pp. 1867–1869.
12. Ibid., Part 7, pp. 2997-2998. The FBI investigated the Moris but never brought any charges.

Chapter 8

7 December 1941

As Oahu slept with most of its defenses at rest, Admiral Nagumo's First Air Fleet arrived at a predesignated point 220 miles north of the island. At 5:30 A.M., the Japanese catapulted a pair of float-reconnaissance aircraft to scout for the U.S. Pacific Fleet. Then the aircraft carriers turned into the wind and began to launch the first wave of attackers at 6 A.M. in the first light of 7 December 1941.

First Lieutenant Kermit Tyler, a pilot with the 78th Pursuit Squadron, was at his assigned post in the information center at Fort Shafter in accordance with Major Bergquist's schedule. Motoring through the quiet streets of Honolulu earlier, he had been aware that a radio station was broadcasting Hawaiian music, uninterrupted by announcements. "I remembered that a bomber pilot friend, Lieutenant Morris Shedd, had told me that the music broadcast was left on all night when a flight of B-17s was being ferried in from the San Francisco area." Indeed, 12 B-17C and E aircraft of the 38th and 88th reconnaissance squadrons from Hamilton Field, California, were closing on the Hawaiian Islands from the northeast.

Tyler was familiar with the information center, having had a similar watch on 3 December. But with only a dozen or so Signal Company enlisted personnel present, he could do no more than go through the motions of familiarizing himself with the amphitheater. The center had been a beehive of activity during the frequent air raid drills of past months, when the radar operators and plotters had practiced locating approaching flights and vectoring fighters to mock intercepts. They had even begun to track approaching flights from the mainland, including the Pan American Clippers. But on this date, Tyler was the only officer present, and there was no activity from 4 A.M. onward.

Forty officers and enlisted men of the Signal Corps Air Warning Company were stationed at Kawailoa on Oahu's north coast near Haleiwa. They manned SCR-270B mobile radar units nearby and on the mountain chain that overlooked the northeast coast of Oahu. Sergeant George Mooney and Private Forrest E. Souder had a shift from midnight to 8 A.M. at the Kawailoa radar. Privates Joseph L. Lockard and George Elliott, with the same early shift at Opana, camped at the remote mountain site the night before.

From prior experience, the army radar technicians were aware that the B-17s from California might be headed for Oahu. They also knew of the navy's routine of flying carrier air groups into Oahu as the flattops returned to port. At 6:45 A.M. the Kawailoa and Opana units picked up an unusual radar target about 60 miles to the north. It was a small radar image, but Mooney, at Kawailoa, attempted to contact the "filter center," a term used by the Signal Corps personnel for the information center at Fort Shafter. There was a phone problem, but Mooney finally got his message through to Private Joseph P. McDonald, who was manning the information center switchboard. This modest radar target caused no alarm, and the contact was tracked until 7:05 A.M., when Kawailoa shut down, and the crew went for breakfast.

That unidentified image on the radar was the pair of Aichi E13A1 "Jake" scouts launched by the heavy cruisers *Chikuma* and *Tone* from the enemy task force. The *Tone*'s aircraft reconnoitered Kaneohe Bay, then Lahina Roads. *Chikuma*'s scout flew down the groin of Oahu and was captured momentarily by Fort Shafter's radar. The scout then proceeded to Pearl Harbor for a last-minute reconnaissance of the Pacific Fleet at anchor.

Tyler recalled, "About the same time the plotters folded up their equipment and left for breakfast. I was surprised because it left only a telephone operator and me on duty."

Just before Kawailoa's radar was secured for the morning, the crew at Opana, high on the northern tip of the Koolau mountain range, received another echo on its radar. The time was 7:02 A.M., and it was a very large image, the biggest either soldier had ever seen. They plotted it at 136 miles, at an azimuth five degrees northeast of their location. With the contact closing south at a distance of 132 miles, Joe Lockard called the information center and spoke with Joe McDonald. McDonald gave the message to Tyler, who seemed disinterested. Tyler said, "A few plots had started appearing in and around the island [navy PBYs], but there seemed to be nothing unusual." At Lockard's insistence, Tyler came on the phone to get the information firsthand. [1]

"The Opana operator said something to the effect that it's the biggest image he had ever seen," Tyler said. Had a navy watch officer, familiar with aircraft carrier operations, been present at the desk, he could have declared instantly that the radar target was not from either *Lexington* or *Enterprise*.

What Tyler did know was that the alert of the previous weeks, where he and fellow pilots had periodically been standing by their aircraft, had been canceled. He also knew that no fighters were ready to scramble at Wheeler. The guns of his own squadron's P-40s had been removed for cleaning. Thus, he dismissed the matter of the Opana radar contact. Lockard and Elliott watched with fascination until 7:39 A.M., when the oncoming image left their oscilloscope. That radar contact, then some 20 miles distant, had been the first wave of the Japanese attack force approaching at 125-miles-per-hour airspeed with a tail wind.

Just as the Aircraft Warning Service radar had unknowingly begun tracking Japanese aircraft, an extraordinary incident occurred off the south coast of Oahu, in the approaches to Pearl Harbor. At 6:30 A.M. the patrolling destroyer *Ward* was summoned to investigate a strange object that seemed to be following the stores ship *Antares*. The *Ward*'s skipper, Lieutenant William Outerbridge, established visual contact, determined that he was looking at an enemy submarine, and attacked with his deck guns, then dropped depth charges as his ship overran the submarine wake. At 6:45 A.M. he radioed to the 14th Naval District that he had ". . . attacked, fired upon, and dropped depth charges upon submarine operating in defensive sea area." [2]

The *Ward*'s message was relayed to Captain John Earle, Bloch's chief of staff, and Lieutenant Commander R.B. Black on Kimmel's staff, promoting a flurry of phone calls between chiefs and subordinates. Meanwhile, Ensign William P. Tanner, a patrolling Catalina pilot from VP-14 who had witnessed the *Ward*'s attack, dropped smoke markers and then made his own attack run with depth charges to where he calculated that the diving sub would be. Tanner's radio message, "Sunk one enemy submarine one mile south of Pearl Harbor," propelled Lieutenant Commander Logan Ramsey to the patrol wing office. But for the rest of the navy command, skepticism seemed the order of the day. [3]

Admiral Kimmel was finally appraised of the navy encounters between 7:30 and 7:40 A.M. He dressed quickly, but neither he nor anyone else in the navy thought to alert the army to these alarming events. Nor did any of his staff on duty in the fleet headquarters over-looking Battleship Row, think to take any action except for ordering the standby destroyer in the harbor, the USS *Monaghan*, to get underway in the event that the *Ward* required assistance. With both a destroyer and a PBY radioing that they had detected and attacked a submarine near the entrance to Pearl Harbor, at least additional destroyers should have been ordered to get up steam, and possibly a fleet-wide submarine alert should have been issued.

As the U.S. Navy began to bestir itself, the first wave of Japanese aircraft was crossing Oahu. Commander Mitsuo Fuchida, leader of the carrier air units, viewed a quiet Pearl Harbor through his binoculars and prepared to deploy his squadrons. He had just heard a favorable weather report, courtesy of KGMB. Then *Chikuma's* scout radioed a confirmation of the ships in the harbor. The sight of the U.S. fleet at anchor and a sky void of interceptors or antiaircraft fire told the Japanese aviators that they had achieved complete surprise.

Logan Ramsey had just arrived at Patrol Wing headquarters when the bombs and torpedoes of the Japanese first wave began detonating. He ran into his Ford Island office to flash a radio warning to all shore stations and ships at sea, one that was destined to shock the world. It was sent in the clear, uncoded: "Air raid Pearl Harbor! This is no drill!"

The Japanese first struck at Pearl Harbor and Naval Air Station Ford Island at 7:45 A.M. Naval Air Station Kaneohe was hit moments later. Wheeler Field and Hickam Field were attacked almost simultaneously minutes before 8 A.M. Despite a state of unpreparedness, personnel of both services rose to the occasion in a courageous ad hoc defense.

At Wheeler, General Davidson was out of his house at the first sound of laboring aircraft engines. He confronted Colonel Bill Flood in the street. "God damn the navy! They're beating us up on Sunday when they know we aren't on practice alert! Bill, can you get the numbers on any of those planes?" Flood answered, "Christ, General, they've got rising suns painted on them!"

Major Ken Bergquist was still in bed listening to the chatter of his four-year-old daughter when he heard what he thought was a navy plane in a screaming power dive. A terrific explosion followed, and Ken said to his wife, "My God, he went in." But as more explosions followed he knew that his worst nightmare had been realized. Still pulling on his clothes, he raced outside to face a strafing enemy aircraft. After getting his wife and child in a closet, he hailed a passing staff car. He had a quick conversation with General Davidson, then started for Fort Shafter, which was 20 miles away. Bergquist vividly recalled the trip:

> Shortly after we left Wheeler we faced a strafing Japanese plane. I said, "Let's get the hell out of here." The driver slid to a stop and he ran for cover. Based on some silly instinct, I stayed in the car and ducked behind the dashboard as bullets spattered all around. The soldier was hit in the leg but gamely returned to the car. I had a finger slashed. We continued on, and a second plane dived and strafed the road but missed us. I spent the next five days at the information center, uncertain of the status of my wife and daughter. It turned out that they were all right.

Wheeler's hangars and other buildings were bombed. Twenty-five attacking Aichi D3A Val dive bombers then set up a gunnery pattern to strafe aircraft, buildings, and anything that moved. They went about their business unmolested, except for a handful of personnel who fired at them with side arms. The mobile antiaircraft batteries assigned to Wheeler Field were parked at adjoining Schofield Barracks, and their ammunition was at another location. Despite the deadly Japanese strafing, officers and enlisted men raced to the hangar line.

One bomb hit the 72nd Pursuit Squadron's tent complex, and it also suffered strafing. The torn and burning tents contained more than two dozen casualties. The squadron commander, First Lieutenant Jim Beckwith, was appalled at the suffering and death among his enlisted men and concentrated his efforts on them. All of his new P-40s were burning and beyond hope.

Lieutenant Norval Heath and two fellow officers, Lieutenants Gus Ahola and Minar Dervage, drove to the edge of the flight line. Ahola attempted to extricate his 19th Squadron P-40 from the blazing line of aircraft on the ramp. He taxied out but could not get any lift at takeoff and discovered his elevator surfaces had been burned through. Heath was also serving as a technical supply officer, and he went into a burning hangar to rescue a valuable speed graphic camera recently entrusted to his care. "It had seemed important at the time," he later reflected. Bent low to see through the smoke, he found General Davidson surveying the damage amidst the fires.

While some personnel attended to the many wounded and dying, others, including Davidson, began to push undamaged aircraft clear of the flight line inferno. A bomb hit Hanger No. 3, where most of the ammunition taken from aircraft on the ramp had been stored. The periodic explosions of these rounds added to the danger. The huge cloud of black smoke from rows of burning fighter planes provided a smoke screen of sorts for the 46th Pursuit Squadron's P-36 aircraft at the south end of the ramp. Those that had been spared early damage were pushed or taxied to revetments even while the strafing continued.

Second Lieutenant Philip Rasmussen buckled a Colt. 45 over his pajamas before he began taxiing his P-36 to a bunker. As Vals roared overhead, he banged away with his pistol in a defiant, but largely futile, manner.

While the attack was underway, pilots from the 47th Pursuit Squadron who were spending the night at Wheeler checked in by telephone with Haleiwa airstrip to see if their planes also had been targeted and destroyed. However, the otherwise impeccable Japanese intelligence had overlooked Haleiwa. The 47th pilots told the officer of the day and ground crews to ready their planes. Then, five of them—Rogers, Brown, Dains, Taylor, and Welch—got into two cars, made a dash for the field on Oahu's northern coast, and were strafed en route.

Major Lorry Tindal was quartered at Hickam Field with his family. The concussion from the first bomb explosion rocked his house, blew down a cover from a ceiling light, and sent his five-year-old screaming into his room. Tindal and his wife bolted from bed, and he dressed hurriedly as his wife tucked her child and a neighbor boy into a walk-in pantry. Arriving at the Fort Shafter Information Center at about 8:30 A.M., Tindal tried to make sense of the many radar images that were being plotted. Kermit Tyler had already recalled all nearby Signal Corps officers and enlisted personnel and ordered that the remote radar units be remanned. Lieutenant Grover White, the information center communications officer, assigned Sergeant Merle Stouffer to stand in for the absent navy liaison officers. Corporal Robert D. Myers took over the phone for an absent antiaircraft artillery officer. Ken Bergquist, after fighting his way through chaotic traffic in Honolulu, arrived just after 10:15 A.M. Lieutenant Commander Bill Taylor made it through the same congestion to the information a few minutes later. [4]

The first two pilots to reach Haleiwa and mount their P-40B fighters were Second Lieutenants George Welch and Ken Taylor. They took off about 8:30 A.M. and headed toward the columns of smoke rising from Pearl Harbor, the funeral pyres of Battleship Row. After contacting the controller at the information center, per their training, they waded into a mix of Val dive bombers and Kate torpedo bombers that had already unleashed their loads on the fleet and were strafing the Marine base at Ewa along the designated Japanese departure route. Welch and Taylor each shot down two of the bombers, damaged two others, then turned back for Wheeler to refuel and rearm.

At about 8:45 A.M., First Lieutenant Lew Sanders, commanding officer of the 46th Pursuit Squadron, led four P-36s from Wheeler Field. The flight consisted of First Lieutenant John Thacker and Second Lieutenants Phil Rasmussen and Gordon Sterling. Sanders contacted the Aircraft Warning Service information center, as he had been trained, and Major Tindal directed him toward Koko Head. Sanders reported as he passed through 8,500 feet, and Tindal responded that there were many "bogies" near Kaneohe and Bellows. Still climbing, the four P-36 fighters turned to that heading and, in a slight dive, spotted enemy aircraft. The system that the high command had obstructed and ignored was working as intended despite their indifference.

The bogies that Sanders saw were second-wave fighters from Japanese carriers that had been assigned to hit Bellows Field and Kaneohe Naval Air Station. Shortly before Mitsubishi Zero fighters began their runs on Bellows, personnel at that field had received word of the Japanese strikes on other stations. Only three pilots and a dozen fighter aircraft of the 44th Pursuit Squadron were at Bellows. Officers and enlisted men raced to the flight line and began readying three P-40s. First Lieutenant George Whiteman was off the runway first and was quickly attacked, shot down, and killed near the beach. Second Lieutenant Hans Christiansen was reaching for his cockpit when a fatal round from a Zero struck him down on the tarmac. First

Lieutenant Sam Bishop managed to get his Tomahawk airborne amidst swarming Zeros, but he was hit repeatedly, lost power, and managed to ditch in the surf off the end of the runway. Although wounded, Bishop swam back to shore.

At this juncture Sanders' flight engaged the Bellows attackers over Kaneohe Bay and claimed to have shot down three, plus one probable. Only one crash was seen, but two Zeros, damaged and leaking gas, made for a rendezvous with submarine *I-74*. One crash-landed on Niihau Island and the other reportedly crashed at sea. [5]

During the Sanders' action, Gordon Sterling was jumped by a Zero and crashed to his death in Kaneohe Bay. Rasmussen's P-36 absorbed more than 400 holes from the machine guns and cannons of Zeros, but he managed to return to Wheeler. Sanders and Rasmussen each claimed one enemy aircraft and thought that Sterling had gotten one. Thacker's guns jammed, but he went through the motions of making dry runs on Japanese fighters.

Meanwhile, Second Lieutenant John Dains had taken off from Haleiwa in a P-40B. He sortied alone and is believed to have had a successful dogfight with a lone Japanese aircraft off the northeast coast of Oahu. Aircraft Warning Service personnel from the Kaaawa radar site observed such an engagement.

Two more 47th Pursuit Squadron officers, First Lieutenant Robert Rogers and Second Lieutenant Harry Brown, departed Haleiwa in P-36s soon after Dains. They flew together, engaging one enemy plane near Kahuku Point that was returning northward. The action was inconclusive and both pilots proceeded west toward Kaena Point. There they ran into heavy Japanese traffic returning to their carriers. Brown downed two and Rogers claimed one as a probable.

Ken Taylor and George Welch were being feverishly rearmed and refueled by ground crews at Wheeler when, at about 9:10 A.M., several enemy aircraft were seen approaching at low altitude from the direction of Pearl Harbor. Still in their P-40 cockpits, the young flyers unhesitatingly took off before servicing had been completed. In the ensuing low-level dogfight, Welch shot down two more enemy aircraft, and Taylor was wounded but managed to land. The Japanese flight was apparently returning north and, because of the sortie by Welch and Taylor, caused no additional damage at Wheeler.

John Dains flew one more solo mission from Haleiwa, and three more pilots from the 46th Squadron became airborne during the attack, taking off individually, engaging the retreating enemy, and damaging two Japanese raiders. They were Lieutenants Malcolm Moore, John Webster, and Othneil Norris. All returned. When the battle was over, John Dains took off once more from Haleiwa destined for Wheeler Field. On his landing approach, while over Schofield Barracks, nervous army troops fired on Dains, and he died when his P-36 crashed.

The day's score for the army fighters, despite having no pilots on alert status and with chaos reigning at their airdromes, was 11 Japanese aircraft shot down, three probables, and two damaged by 14 pilots, evidence of how a fully alerted command might have disrupted an attacking force. Fourteenth Pursuit Wing pilot losses in combat were Christiansen, Dains, Sterling, and Whiteman.

At the three army fighter fields there had been 84 pursuit planes in operating condition and 60 in repair status at the start of the attack. [6] Destruction and damage on the ground had been so extensive that, had the Japanese rearmed their first wave and sent it back for another strike, only 38 P-36 and P-40 fighters would have been available to counter the blow. However, this was nearly three times the number that actually sortied against the first two waves and would, no doubt, have made it a costly battle for the third attack wave. Three hundred and fifty-four Japanese aircraft had been involved in the two-wave raid. The attackers lost 29 to flak and fighters and some 21 additional damaged aircraft were considered unsalvageable upon return to the Japanese carriers. [7]

In the excitement of combat, only a few of the 14th Pursuit Wing pilots communicated with and were controlled by the information center early in the day. As operations became more organized, combat air patrols were put up and searches were flown by the handful of 18th Bomb Wing aircraft that had escaped destruction. Most of these flights were controlled by the center. Throughout the remainder of 7 December, the center directed interceptions that chased perceived bogies and, in one case, a suspicious early evening light that turned out to be a rising Venus.

The communications, the numerous plots, and the varied directions of aircraft had nearly overwhelmed the few people on duty at the information center. There were plots developed from the two Japanese strike waves and then plots from retiring attackers, the latter seeming to go southwest but actually rounding the southwest tip of Oahu at Barbers Point, and turning north for a pre-established rendezvous point at sea 20 miles and bearing 340 degrees from Kaena Point. [8] Then there were the overlapping plots of the few Army Air Force fighters, and a flight of 18 *Enterprise* squadrons VB-6 and VS-6 Douglas SBD Dauntless dive bombers that arrived during the attack. The latter were returning to Ford Island totally unaware of the attack. They were savaged by Japanese aircraft and fired at by "friendly" antiaircraft crews. Six of the 18 SBDs were shot down or crash-landed with a loss of eight air crew members. [9]

The B-17s approaching from California also added to the radar echoes, flying in individually, some very near the approach bearing of the Japanese attackers. They arrived during the battle, landing all over the Island of Oahu: eight at Hickam, one at Bellows, two at Haleiwa, and one on Kahuku golf course. It was not until some days later, when the various radar plots could be analyzed, that the early tracks of the Japanese scout and the first wave of attackers became fully apparent to senior commanders. However, Aircraft Warning Service personnel and pilots aloft on 7 December 1941 knew that the Japanese fleet must be to the north.

After Lew Sanders had refueled and rearmed, he led another flight of P-36s from Wheeler and attempted to place a combat air patrol over Pearl Harbor. However, army and navy antiaircraft gunners, still not linked to the Aircraft Warning Service by liaison officers, could not or would not control their heavy batteries, and Sanders was forced to withdraw after being subjected to an infuriating barrage at 12,000 feet. Two P-36s received minor flak damage.

The final disaster of this terrible day occurred when six Grumman F4F Wildcats of VF-6 flew from the *Enterprise* to Ford Island that evening. They radioed ahead, were advised by the Ford Island tower to approach from a specified direction, and word went out by radio to ships in the harbor to expect the incoming fighters. At approximately 9 P.M., the six aircraft, with landing gear and flaps extended and running lights burning brightly, passed over the perimeter of Pearl Harbor. Jumpy gunners on the heavy cruiser *New Orleans* fired first, and then other ships joined in. Four of the Wildcats were shot down, and two managed to land on Ford Island. Three pilots were killed. Had the Aircraft Warning Service controlled antiaircraft batteries on ship and ashore, as had been requested earlier, this final tragic episode would have been averted. [10]

Some navy antiaircraft batteries were manned from the first minutes of the attack as crew members fought gallantly to defend their ships. However, the only army units that responded promptly were those in fixed locations. The many mobile batteries had to draw ammunition from storage depots at Schofield Barracks and Aliamanu Crater and proceed to their assigned locations. This process, in some cases, was completed long after the attack had ended. [11]

Since all ship and shore antiaircraft batteries were finally alerted, provided with ammunition, and had honed their skills against on the first two attack waves, and since the remaining army pursuits were manned and spoiling for a crack at the enemy, a third attack wave of Japanese aircraft would have taken very heavy losses. Despite losses, had the Japanese concentrated their attacks not on ships but fuel storage, dry docks, and machine shops, the Pacific Fleet might have been sent packing back to the West Coast. It was perhaps one of the great blunders of World War II that Admiral Nagumo was content with the deadly, though limited, results already achieved. Pearl Harbor remained as the key logistic and repair base for the Pacific Fleet, and all of the sunk and damaged ships, except for the battleships *Arizona* and *Oklahoma,* lived to fight another day.

On 8 December, inter-service cooperation magically became the norm at the Aircraft Warning Service information center, according to Ken Bergquist: "Our orphaned operation was suddenly everyone's favorite stepchild. I could get anything I wanted. All I had to do was snap my fingers."

That day the navy accepted that the center would control all air traffic and all antiaircraft fire from either shore batteries or ship's guns. And finally, the long sought-after navy liaison watch officers for the information center materialized. There were 10 of them, all from the battleship *California,* which had been sunk at its moorings alongside Ford Island. Navy officers continued to man navy liaison posts from that time until the end of World War II. [12]

Despite the failures of the command structure to properly employ its men and equipment in an alert defense of the fleet and Oahu, scores of junior officers and enlisted men from all services acted with courage and initiative in the face of the surprise attack. For decades, a plaque in the Wheeler Field officers' club exemplified the attitude of the airmen. It said simply, "Never Again."

1. Army Pearl Harbor Board, Part 27, pp. 522–524.

2. Hewitt Inquiry, Part 36, p. 57.

3. Naval Historical Center, War Diary of Patrol Squadron 14.

4. Joint Congressional Committee, Part 19, pp. 3638–3640.

5. Niihau Island, with a population of 180 persons, was isolated from the other Hawaiian islands, without radio, telephones, or even electricity. The Zero pilot, who found a lone sympathizer of Japan ancestry, had a few days of heady freedom, during which he terrorized others, before he was killed in a fight with another islander.

6. Roberts Commission, Part 24, pp. 1763–1765.

7. Joint Congressional Committee, Part 13, Exhibit of Commander Mitsuo Fuchida interrogation, pp. 406–408.

8. Ibid., p. 409.

9. Roberts Commission, Part 24, pp. 1393-1394.

10. Ibid.

11. Joint Congressional Committee, Part 1, p. 55.

12. Hart Inquiry, Part 26, p. 383.

Part II

The Case for Dereliction

Chapter 9

The Failure to Search

The war warning of 27 November 1941 had ordered General Short and Admiral Kimmel to "conduct reconnaissance." Their failure to do so was not for lack of long-range aircraft, as they later testified. On the morning of 7 December 1941—prior to the Japanese attack—the following multi-engine aircraft, all with some long-range capability, were available at Oahu's various airfields, not counting those in repair or maintenance:

	Inventory	Effective Radius *
Navy Patrol Wings 1 and 2		
Consolidated PBY Catalinas airborne	7	750
At Kaneohe and Ford Island	54	750
Navy Utility Squadrons		
VJ-1 and VMJ-252 at Ford Island and Ewa		
Sikorsky JRS-1	12	387
Hawaiian Air Force		
Boeing B-17D	6	700

Douglas B-18	21	500
Sikorsky OA-8	1	400
Total	101	

> * One-half maximum range. To express range, the navy used nautical miles and the Army Air Force statute miles. The numbers used in this volume are as the services used them. [1]

In addition, there were six army Douglas A-20A bombers of lesser range, several Grumman JRF amphibians, and about 100 single-engine aircraft, army O-47s, navy J2Fs, SOCs, and OS2Us, and Marine SBDs and SB2Us that could have been used for "in-shore" patrol, which was not more than 20 miles from Oahu (see Appendixes D, E, and F). Employment of these idle aircraft would have relieved PBYs from anti-submarine patrol in the approaches to Pearl Harbor. After the attack, when circumstances finally compelled army and navy decision makers to do the best with what they had at hand, all aircraft types not destroyed or seriously damaged were pressed into service in the desperate hope of locating the enemy fleet or hunting lurking submarines.

The bulk of the army's distant reconnaissance force would have been the B-18s, which General Martin was disdainful of. Two of his units, the 4th and the 50th reconnaissance squadrons, had trained at the task. Absent a bomb load and cruising at 167 miles per hour at 10,000 feet, the B-18 had six and a half hours of flight capability, or an operating radius of more than 500 miles. Yet, in his post-attack testimony, Martin steadfastly maintained that their range was only 300 miles. As the Army Pearl Harbor Board of 1944 persisted in questioning General Martin about the lack of a reconnaissance effort, Martin conceded that the B-18s, although unable to adequately protect themselves, had a search capability: "They could be used for reconnaissance, but you would lose them as fast as you sent them out, if you sent them into combat." [2]

The navy's PBY flying boats were only a little better equipped to defend themselves (four machine guns compared to the B-18's three) and were slower (178 miles per hour at maximum speed and 100 miles per hour at cruising speed). Again, Martin's unwillingness to operate with anything but his hypothetical force of 180 Boeing B-17s was manifest.

The effort to discredit the capability of the B-18 continued at the 1944 Army Pearl Harbor Board when Colonel James Mollison, Martin's chief of staff, testified. He championed the unsuitability of the B-18 for reconnaissance, noting that there was no window in these planes for vertical observation of the water. Mollison, however, was referring to anti-submarine missions, not reconnaissance for an approaching enemy surface armada. [3] While the B-18 did not have the side blisters of the PBY for observers, its pilots and nose observer had as much visibility as a PBY crew did from similar stations. World War II is replete with the critical location of the enemy by lone PBY crews as well, the most notable example being the sighting of the German battleship *Bismarck* in May 1941 and the Japanese fleet at the Battle of Midway in June 1942.

Martin's utopian 360-degree search plan became one of Admiral Kimmel's crutches. In his 1955 autobiographical defense, Kimmel stated: "A search of all sectors of approach to an island base is the only type of search that deserves the name." [4] Kimmel clung to this assertion despite the fact that the Joint Defense Plan recognized that a Japanese naval force would not have unlimited avenues of approach for a carrier strike. Bellinger and Martin had considered the problems of the enemy fleet in possible routes, the distance those courses might take, and the risk of detection by both naval surface units and merchant shipping. In his 20 August 1941 assessment to Army Air Force headquarters in Washington—the plea for 180 B-17s—Martin had stated that the "most probable" direction for a Hawaiian attack would be from the two western quadrants, from 180 to 360 degrees. [5]

As time passed, Hawaii's air leaders were forced to consider most likely options. According to Commander Ramsey, the most dangerous sector had been refined to 315 to 360 degrees, the area that the Japanese fleet actually approached from. [6]

Rear Admiral John H. Newton, testifying before the Hart Inquiry in April 1944, supported this thesis. He stated that he felt that any Japanese attack on Oahu would come from the north rather than the busy sea lanes and U.S. Navy training exercise areas to the south. [7]

Three task forces were operating to the southwest and west of Hawaii during the period after the 27 November 1941 war warning. Task Force 3, one cruiser and six destroyer-mine sweepers, went southwest to Johnston Island on an amphibious training mission. The *Enterprise* task force was headed almost due west to Wake Island. The *Lexington* task force was bound for Midway, west-northwest of Oahu. Both of the aircraft carriers were conducting routine, 200-mile air searches as they steamed. PBYs operating between Wake and Midway searched from Oahu to Johnston, from Johnston to Midway, and then around the perimeter of Midway. The Wake Island PBY squadron searched on its return to Oahu. By Admiral Kimmel's own estimate, these units had scoured about 2 million square miles just prior to the attack. In addition to these forces, U.S. submarines were conducting patrols near Midway and Wake. Kimmel testified that from Monday, 1 December, through Thursday, 4 December, Bellinger's patrol squadrons searched north and northwest of Oahu to a distance of 400 miles, then the PBYs and their crews stood down for maintenance and rest. [8]

Admiral Bellinger had estimated that 18 patrol aircraft flying sectors five degrees apart could scout 144 degrees of the compass. A joint undertaking by the army and navy's collective force of 101 long-range aircraft could have continued to scout north and northwest for a considerable period, providing relief to each other's crews and aircraft. If nothing else, the army aircraft could have relieved the navy of the shorter range anti-submarine patrols. However, the top Hawaiian air officers, despite their collaboration on the joint defense plan, were not sufficiently motivated by the imminence of war to modify their peacetime procedures. None of the principle commanders even discussed the possibility of an ad hoc joint search operation.

Expanding the long-range search group to include available navy and army multi-engine aircraft would have required that those air crews be let in on certain intelligence. What were they supposed to be looking for? Missing Japanese carrier divisions constituted a clear and present danger to Oahu. Since Kimmel and Short were not comparing such vital intelligence with each other—or Short was ignoring what was shared—neither of them were motivated to disclose it to the rank and file.

At the various Pearl Harbor investigative hearings, the senior commanders continued to justify their actions. Martin lamented that he had only six aircraft with long-range search capability, the B-17Ds. Under probing by Lieutenant General George Grunert, the president of the Army Pearl Harbor Board, Martin was asked if he did not have an obligation to make the best use of what he had. He gave a convoluted response finally indicating that he had only planned to use the 180 B-17s he had hoped for and not the mix of aircraft he in fact had in December 1941. [9]

Further, Martin felt little obligation to perform reconnaissance, as he assumed that the navy was conducting the chore. [10] He also assumed that navy task forces at sea would help with distant reconnaissance and provide warning. They did patrol in a wide arc around and ahead of both carrier task forces, searching for submarines as well as surface ships. But the *Enterprise* and *Lexington* task forces were generally west of the Hawaiian Islands. [11]

The commander of Martin's bomber forces, Brigadier General Jacob Rudolph, was of no help to his superior in the matter of reconnaissance to protect the fortress. He believed that the Japanese would not "dare" to attack Oahu; therefore he saw no need to use his aircraft on search missions. He, too, thought that the navy was conducting some reconnaissance with their Catalinas, but interestingly, he stated that he had, "no confidence in flying boats." [12]

Rear Admiral Bellinger acknowledged that part of the Pacific Fleet Operating Plan was to guard Oahu against surprise attack by the Japanese. But he saw his primary mission as the preservation of the patrol squadrons for service to the fleet when it sortied. [13] In his defense, Bellinger was not advised of the war warning by Kimmel or Bloch. He only knew what he could "glean" from the newspapers. [14] However, he had participated in a mock U.S. carrier strike on Pearl Harbor in 1938 and was concerned about the possibility of a surprise air raid. [15]

Bellinger testified to a later investigative panel that he believed the joint defense plan was doomed to failure because it lacked unity and would go into effect only when an emergency was declared. It was also his recollection that the Aircraft Warning Service information center was not operational and that the AWS personnel were reluctant to have air raid drills. [16]

Bellinger's operations officer, Commander Logan Ramsey, testified that for an emergency effort some 60 PBYs could have been made available on four-hour notice. [17] Captain Arthur Davis, the fleet aviation officer, conceded that distant reconnaissance could have been done on a limited basis with army cooperation. [18]

Like his subordinate Major General Martin, General Short believed that navy task forces provided him with a degree of security, although he confessed to knowing little of the navy's comings and goings. He assumed that the navy was providing distant air reconnaissance, beyond 20 miles, but was ignorant as to numbers of aircraft and the frequency of searches. He stated that he was not kept advised of this information by the navy. Still he trusted that the navy would give him warning of an impending air attack. [19] Before the Roberts Commission, Kimmel disputed Short's claim that the army was uninformed concerning navy task force activity, saying that ship operating schedules had been routinely provided to the army's Hawaiian Department headquarters prior to the attack. [20]

Lieutenant General George Grunert asked Short, "Did it not occur to you that the war warning necessitated a state of war readiness?" Short responded that he counted on the navy to prevent a Japanese task force from getting through. "If they [officials in Washington] had been expecting an air attack, they should have said so." [21]

With regard to the war warning's directive to undertake reconnaissance, Short stated before the Army Pearl Harbor Board in 1944 that he interpreted the order as a lack of familiarity within the War Department of the Joint Hawaiian Coastal Defense Agreement. The navy, he said, had that responsibility. [22] Short still maintained that he had only six B-17s available for reconnaissance, and that the Hawaiian Air Force had an obligation under the Joint Defense Agreement to conserve its bomber strength for the contingency of an attack on an enemy fleet. He apparently was referring to the B-18s that he and Martin considered useless. [23]

For his part, Admiral Kimmel testified before the Roberts Commission that the periodic joint air raid drills were dress rehearsals for a raid he did not expect. He considered air attack possible although not probable. Therefore, he did not discuss air defense with General Short, as it was, "an army responsibility." [24]

Before the subsequent Navy Court of Inquiry, Kimmel said that he had approved the limited distant reconnaissance operating plans for the patrol wings, although at the war warning meeting with Short and Admiral Bloch on 28 November, the consensus was that a Pearl Harbor attack was, "a remote possibility." [25]

By about 11 A.M. on 7 December, the navy and Hawaiian Air Force had managed to implement the joint search effort that they had scorned prior to the attack. They cobbled together a force of five B-17s, three B-18s, a pair of A-20s, 13 PBYs, two JRS-1s, six OS2Us, nine SBDs, and six Grumman J2Fs (one of them armed only with a rifle). These 46 aircraft fanned out to search for the Japanese fleet, with army fighters escorting some missions. As these survivors of the raid became serviceable, they set off individually or in small groups to reconnoiter agreed sectors up to 300 miles from Oahu. [26]

But after recovering its aircraft, the Japanese task force had retired northward at high speed and was never sighted. Similar joint search efforts were undertaken for several days following the attack. Much of the initial search was wasted toward the south, as the navy followed what Wilfred Tetley called, "their orange instincts," (looking toward the Japanese mandated islands of the southwest). None of the senior commanders, army or navy, sought any clues from the information center regarding its early radar contacts with the approaching Japanese strike aircraft until the following day.

Besides his patrol wings, Kimmel also possessed another long-range scouting force: the dozen submarines based at Pearl Harbor. Four were in Pearl Harbor for maintenance and replenishment. Eight were at sea, of which four were patrolling off Wake and Midway on what Kimmel described as "war patrols." None was deployed to patrol north of Oahu for the possible approach of a Japanese strike force. [27]

In contrast, the Japanese employed 27 fleet submarines in advance of the carrier strike force. Five carried the midget submarines that were to sneak into Pearl Harbor and each add its two torpedoes to the carnage. The others were engaged in reconnaissance for the First Air Fleet and as a blockade of channels between the various Hawaiian Islands; one was stationed at a predesignated point south of Niihau Island with the additional duty to rescue air crews. All were prepared to engage U.S. warships that might survive the Japanese surprise attack and put to sea. [28]

In the final analysis, both commands took a rest on Saturday, 6 December 1941, and Sunday, 7 December, and 71 of the aircraft with long- and medium-range reconnaissance capability were destroyed on the ground or at their moorings in Kaneohe Bay. Whether a search effort on 6 and 7 December would have found the enemy task force, or even its first strike formation winging toward Oahu, is problematic. Available hours of daylight and weather conditions would have posed limits to observation. And whether or not such a sighting, coupled with *Ward*'s stunning message and that of Tanner's PBY regarding an encounter with a submarine, would have awakened the slumbering Hawaiian defense system is also uncertain. But the absence of any joint army-navy effort to search for an enemy based on a lack of search aircraft is indefensible. Because of the fog of misinformation spread by witnesses and the lack of technical knowledge among investigative panelists, the issue of suitable, available reconnaissance aircraft was never pursued in the various hearings.

1. Source of *Aircraft Inventory*: Roberts Commission, Part 24, Exhibit T, p. 1833; Hart Inquiry, Part 26, pp. 122–133, and Naval Historical Center, Washington, D.C. Source of Range Data: Naval Historical Center, USAF Museum Archives Gallery, aircraft performance data; and W. F. Craven and J. L. Cate, *The Army Air Forces in World War II*, Vol. I, p. 748.

2. Army Pearl Harbor Board, Part 28, p. 973–989.

3. Ibid., Part 27, pp. 422–423.

4. Husband E. Kimmel, *Admiral Kimmel's Story*, p. 66.

5. Joint Congressional Committee, Part 1, p. 393.

6. Navy Court of Inquiry, Part 32, p. 452.

7. Hart Inquiry, Part 26, p. 347.

8. Husband E. Kimmel, *Admiral Kimmel's Story*, pp. 63–65.

9. Army Pearl Harbor Board, Part 28, pp. 987-989.

10. Roberts Commission, part 23, p. 997.

11. Army Pearl Harbor Board, Part 28, p. 972.

12. Ibid., Part 27, p. 638.

13. Hewitt Inquiry, Part 36, p. 284–286.

14. Roberts Commission, Part 22, p. 565.

15. Ibid., pp. 562–565.

16. Hart Inquiry, Part 26, pp. 122–137.

17. Navy Court of Inquiry, Part 32, p. 451.

18. Hart Inquiry, Part 26, pp. 106–109.

19. Army Pearl Harbor Board, Part 27, pp. 192–209.

20. Roberts Commission, Part 23, pp. 897–898.

21. Army Pearl Harbor Board, Part 27, p. 226.

22. Ibid., pp. 160-161.

23. Ibid., pp. 171-172.

24. Roberts Commission, Part 22, pp. 387–390.

25. Navy Court of Inquiry, Part 32, p. 289.

26. Roberts Commission, Part 24, p. 1607.

27. Joint Congressional Committee, Part 21, Item 15, "Disposition of U.S. Pacific Fleet on 7 December 1941."

28. David C. Evans, *The Japanese Navy In World War II*, pp. 25–28.

Chapter 10

The Failure to Defend

Kimmel-Short apologists contend that the failure to conduct distant reconnaissance was the result of both limited resources and a Washington intelligence conspiracy that skewed the judgment of Hawaii's top commanders. No such argument can explain their failure to conduct an air defense.

The army's Hawaiian Department had been equipped with considerable antiaircraft artillery, 148 land-based fighter aircraft, six mobile radar units, and an Aircraft Warning Service (AWS) to coordinate the lot. In addition, more than four dozen navy warships mounted scores of antiaircraft guns, from .30-caliber to five-inch. When the Japanese air attack came, the air defense was absent because of the failure of Kimmel-Short and their subordinates to activate the apparatus that was available to them.

To his dying day, General Short would argue that the war warning had led him to believe that there was no real war peril in his part of the world, but rather an inherent sabotage menace. Indeed, 30 percent of the Hawaiian Islands' population, or 160,000 men, women, and children, were of Japanese descent. There were 35,000 Japanese nationals among them and certainly some Japanese sympathizers, but the vast majority tended to be hard-working members of the multicultural community. There were never any indications that these people were belligerent, nor was there a single act of sabotage associated with the Japanese population. Most were assimilated and became U.S. citizens, particularly the second-generation Nisei.

Yet Short, whose primary mission was to protect the fleet and Pearl Harbor, claimed that he feared an uprising on Oahu against his two well-armed infantry divisions and the other 30,000 army personnel more than he feared an air attack from outside the fortress. Even if this judgment was justified, ships of the fleet and the naval base were not easy targets for saboteurs. Yet he declared an end to the long-standing Alert No. 2, against air attack, and instituted Alert No. 1 for anti-sabotage, a lower state of readiness (despite the incongruity of ranking), sending troops to guard vital installations such as bridges and public utilities. The navy had already mounted a sabotage alert at the ground accesses to Pearl Harbor and was not in need of army troops.

At Hickam Field the bombers were bunched on the hangar line. Fighter aircraft at Wheeler Field were moved from their protective bunkers, and they were ganged together before the hangars and their ammunition was removed. Pilots and some ground crews were allowed to stand down after review on 6 December. Army Air Forces enlisted personnel who stood guard on the Hickam and Wheeler ramps and at Haleiwa and Bellows. On the latter three airfields, 84 P-40 and P-36 fighters were available for use, although most were unarmed and many lacked full fuel tanks. [1]

General Martin, co-author of the air defense plan, mirrored Short's preoccupation with sabotage. Long after the attack he claimed that Japanese-American saboteurs with clandestine mobile radios were jamming air frequencies and sending false messages from the time of the attack and for several days thereafter until FBI agents found them. The bureau detected no such activity. [2]

As disastrous as Short's change in focus proved to be, the air defense had been a long-term victim of official obstruction, indifference, buck passing, and a lack of intra- and inter-service cooperation. All of the general and flag officers in Hawaii insisted that they worshipped at the altar of cooperation. But it was a lack of cooperation at senior levels that doomed the air defense of Oahu. Kimmel and Short stated that they met frequently and worked together. Indeed, their relationship was pleasant. During the Army Pearl Harbor Board hearings, General George Grunert posed a rhetorical question on whether ". . . cordial relations between Kimmel and Short caused a delicacy as to interest in one another's affairs that never really got down to the details of your respective responsibilities and inquired into each other's business." [3]

Indeed, Kimmel never inspected the information center of the AWS, and therefore, did not educate himself on its function. [4] He explained his lack of interest, by saying ". . . it was an army responsibility." [5]

Ignorance of the other command's activity is further evidenced from the meetings regarding the war warning messages. Kimmel's units went on an alert that was different from that ordered by Short. Neither was aware of what the other had done, as neither service knew the other's alert system priority numbers. [6]

Short's own command, however, was initially responsible for delaying activation of the AWS. The Army Signal Corps was supposed to get the Aircraft Warning Service built and operating and then relinquish it to the Hawaiian Air Force. Colonel James Mollison, Martin's chief of staff, testified (as Martin would not) regarding the turf war: "There was a lot of bickering and wrangling about control of the AWS. Powell [signal officer] did not want to give them up." [7]

Colonel Powell denied the charge. Yet in his testimony he evidenced little interest in the AWS and never worked to get navy cooperation in providing liaison officers, feeling that it was General Davidson's responsibility as head of the Aircraft Warning Service, even though Powell had resisted relinquishing control of AWS crews and equipment to Davidson. [8]

Even General Short conceded that Aircraft Warning Service equipment was operational at the time the war warning was received on 27 November. But the Signal Corps maintained its grip, and Short planned to implement the transfer on Davidson's return from the mainland on 4 December. With the leisurely pace that had become customary in the army's Hawaiian Department, that transition never occurred until forced by the events of 7 December. [9]

There are those who claim Kimmel and Short were victims of Washington's failures to inform them of critical intelligence. The same charge can be leveled at Hawaii's top commanders. Through their inept administration, they left the War and Navy departments with the belief that progress was being made in the preparation of Oahu's defenses. As air raid drills continued and the air defense system sharpened its skills, General Martin told General Arnold by letter of 25 September that he had five mobile radar sites established, and with the information center nearing completion, he said that the AWS would be "operating within 30 days." [10] However, the "completion" dragged on with Powell's obstruction and the absence of any intervention by his superior, General Short.

General Martin allowed similar obdurate behavior by his subordinate, General Rudolph, who testified he knew nothing about the AWS and could not be cajoled into providing bomber command officers as liaison. Ken Bergquist was told that the bomb wing, which did little practice bombing and did not provide long-range reconnaissance, could not spare any officers because they were too busy training. [11]

Later in his Army Pearl Harbor Board testimony, Rudolph stated that he had more pilots than airplanes, making his refusal to provide bomb wing officers as liaisons at the information center all the more extraordinary. No members of the investigating committee pursued this contradiction, if indeed they caught it. [12]

During the joint army-navy drills between September and November 1941, the navy liaison desks overlooking the plotting board at the information center were always manned by army personnel acting as surrogates for navy representatives. It was all pretend. The actors at the navy liaison posts knew nothing of the location of various naval air units.

Despite the efforts of Lieutenant Commander Bill Taylor, no senior naval officers were willing to assign liaison officers or intervene with Admiral Kimmel. Major Ken Bergquist, one of the few army officers to speak his mind at the various investigative hearings, said that there was no cooperation from the navy and very little from department headquarters (Short's office). [13]

When General Davidson returned to Hawaii on 4 December, he made one last futile effort to gain navy cooperation with Bellinger's office. [14]

Testifying before the many Pearl Harbor investigations, U.S. Navy officers consistently denied that they failed to cooperate while giving responses that disclosed either evasiveness or astonishing ignorance. Admiral Bloch professed that he was unaware of the status of the AWS and knew nothing of its need for navy liaison watch officers, but then noted that he had assigned Lieutenant Harold Burr as a liaison. Burr had been detailed to attend periodic meetings of the joint air defense committee, which was a development board. [15] In a bit of Sophoclean logic, Bloch said during the investigation that the Aircraft Warning Service needed liaison officers when it was established ". . . but the system wasn't established until 7 December 1941." [16]

Members of Kimmel's staff displayed an astonishing lack of awareness of matters that they should have understood with regard to the air defense system. Captain Walter S. DeLany, fleet operations officer, thought that the AWS only had three radars and no appurtenances or equipment needed to make up a system of an information center. [17] Commander Maurice E. Curts, fleet communications officer, believed that the Aircraft Warning Service was not in ". . . an operating status prior to 7 December 1941." And he was one of the rare navy officers who attended infrequent meetings of the air defense committee. [18]

Captain Arthur C. Davis, fleet aviation officer, did not believe that the Aircraft Warning Service was "fully developed," although he acknowledged that there had been drills. He added that he kept Kimmel updated on the progress of the project. [19] Long after the attack, Rear Admiral Bellinger expressed extraordinary views, considering that he was one of the officers who resisted in providing cooperation toward the assignment of liaison watch officers. Regarding the joint defense plans, he told the Hart Inquiry:

> It was based on too much cooperation and also on the assumption that it would go into effect when an emergency arose, and no organization of this kind is any good unless it functions 24 hours per day prior to any air attack, completely and fully manned. And there were insufficient personnel, actually in my estimation, to have such an organization functioning that way. [20]

During questioning by General Walter H. Frank, Admiral Kimmel displayed his confusion regarding the manning of the remote radar units versus the staffing of the information center, but in the matter of liaison officers, his proof of cooperation was the loan of Lieutenant Commander Taylor to the army. He then made the astounding statement that after later learning that the radar stations had picked up the early approach tracks of Japanese attackers, he " . . . felt let down because that was information we wanted above everything else." [21]

Kimmel's complaint is disingenuous. Neither he nor any member of his staff ever called the information center to inquire about what information it might possess. Nor did they contact the 14th Pursuit Wing to determine what they might have gleaned from pilots who had pursued the Japanese raiders. In addition, the navy under Kimmel's leadership was apparently not structured in a way to advise its commander in chief about several incidents that provided circumstantial evidence, if not definitive intelligence, regarding the location of Japanese naval forces:

1. Among the radio messages flying through the ether on 7 December 1941, the navy intercepted homing requests between Japanese pilots and their ships. The bearings of those signals were estimated to be 338 degrees, or north-northwest of Oahu. [22]

2. A pair of SOC-1 scout aircraft from the cruiser Northampton (part of Task Force 8) were attacked by a Zero near Kauai, west-northwest of Oahu. This may have been one of the Japanese fighters that eventually went down near Niihau Island. [23]

3. Ensign Theodore W. Marshall of VP-21 climbed into a Douglas TBD-1 at Ford Island on his own initiative and tracked the Japanese attackers as they disappeared to the north. After 150 miles, he had to return to Oahu because he was low on fuel. [24]

4. Ensign Otto F. Meyer, commanded one of three VP-14 PBYs airborne south of Oahu on anti-submarine duty. After the attack began, he was directed to patrol in an effort to locate the enemy carrier task force. About 10 A.M., north of Oahu, he encountered several Zero fighters that made a brief passing attack on his aircraft then proceeded north. A Japanese officer interviewed by historian Gordon Prange states that a detachment from aircraft carrier Hiryu fired at a flying boat they believed was "trailing them." It seems probable that this was Meyer who ultimately felt obliged to return his damaged aircraft to Kaneohe. [25]

5. One of the few undamaged long-range aircraft available at Ford Island Naval Air Station after the attack was a JRS-1 (navy version of a Sikorsky S-43 transport) of Utility Squadron One. The unarmed flying boat commanded by Lieutenant Wesley H. Ruth was sent aloft to scout for the Japanese fleet. During a five-hour mission north of Oahu, Ruth did not see the enemy task force but came close enough to be briefly engaged by Japanese Zeroes from the fleet's combat air patrol. [26]

Kimmel and his senior officers wanted radar for their ships because it represented a technological leap beyond binoculars in a crow's nest. Radar linked to a combat information center had just recently been installed in a handful of Pacific Fleet warships. It was all new gadgetry that the officers understood only conceptually. However, none of the admirals or their staffs had served a watch in radar-equipped ships to learn the working mechanics of the integrated system. This may explain their apparent ignorance of or indifference to the potential of the army's radar-equipped Aircraft Warning Service.

However, the greatest sinner against the activation of a fully operational Aircraft Warning Service was the man who had campaigned for it, General Short. Although he considered it critical to his air defense mission, he never sought to understand the process. His testimony shows that he regarded the radar as akin to the legendary caged-bird in the coal mine. It was, he seemed to believe, a contrivance that would warn of danger and provide protection regardless of information center manning or the state of readiness of the reaction force, his 14th Pursuit Wing.

It was Short who ordered his own fighter squadrons off alert status and into a normal training mode when he declared the sabotage alert. He simultaneously ordered that the radar units and the information center should be operated from 4 to 7 A.M. on 7 December 1941. His 150-mile-range radar units were only able to detect aircraft within an hour's flying time from Oahu. Yet his interceptors, pilots, and ground crews were placed on four-hour notice. [27]

General Short's testimony before the Army Pearl Harbor Board in 1944 displayed his confusion. He said that the 14th Pursuit Wing was functioning and coordinating with the information center, but that the order had not yet been issued to place the Aircraft Warning Service under Davidson's command, which would have made it really operational. (This assumes that a full complement of watch officers had been available.) He was, however, uncertain about whether the navy had detailed liaison officers, but again mentioned Taylor and Burr. [28]

Short consistently testified that because the War Department did not warn of "imminent air attack," his command was not "alerted for AA defense or probable air attack." Although again claiming that the Aircraft Warning Service was operating, he said that his aircraft were not in readiness because they were being "protected" from sabotage. None of the various investigating committee members thought to ask him why fighters lined up on the Wheeler Field hangar line, under guard, could not still be on alert with crews standing ready. Nor did anyone point out the contradiction that the mere operation of radar sets did not constitute an integrated, working air raid warning and defense system. [29]

A few days after the attack, Short said that Kermit Tyler, the lone watch officer at the information center, might have thought the early morning radar contacts represented one of three things: U.S. Navy carrier air groups, bombers from Hickam Field, or bombers arriving from the mainland. [30] By the time of the 1946 joint congressional committee hearings, Short had changed his tune and made an unseemly attempt to shift blame onto Kermit Tyler:

> What I meant is he [Tyler] had full authority, in spite of the fact that he was a lieutenant, as control officer, had full authority to alert the planes at Wheeler Field. He would just turn them out for hostile planes approaching. If they had received that report, no matter whether it had any value or not, they would have turned out immediately. [31]

This accusation disregards the fact, known to Tyler but still lost on Short, that the interceptors at Wheeler were not manned. Nor were any crews on standby alert, the weekend holiday being a result of the general's orders.

General Davidson, commanding the 14th Pursuit Wing, stated that Tyler would have required a "fifth sense" to "divine" that the radar contacts were Japanese. [32]

1. Roberts Commission, Part 22, p. 102, and Part 24, pp. 1763–1765.

2. Army Pearl Harbor Board, Part 28, pp. 996-997.

3. Ibid., pp. 932-933.

4. Ibid., pp. 934–936.

5. Navy Court of Inquiry, Part 32, pp. 228-229.

6. Army Pearl Harbor Board, Part 28, pp. 928-929.

7. Ibid., Part 27, p. 424.

8. Ibid., Part 29, pp. 1993–1996.

9. Roberts Commission, Part 23, p. 980.

10. Army Pearl Harbor Board, Part 28, p. 981.

11. Ibid., Part 27, p. 630.

12. Ibid., p. 641.

13. Ibid., pp. 618-619.

14. Roberts Commission, Part 22, p. 999.

15. Ibid., pp. 466–469.

16. Navy Court of Inquiry, Part 32, p. 301.

17. Army Pearl Harbor Board, Part 28, pp. 898-899.

18. Hart Inquiry, Part 26, p. 117.

19. Ibid., p. 107.

20. Army Pearl Harbor Board, Part 28, pp. 934–936.

21. Hart Inquiry, Part 26, pp. 128-129.

22. Roberts Commission, Part 24, p. 1599.

23. Naval Historical Center, Engagement report of *Northampton* air crews, RG 38.

24. Robert J. Cressman and J. Michael Wenger, "This Is No Drill," *Naval Aviation News*, November-December, 1991.

25. Patrol Wing 1, VP-14 diary of 7 December 1941, and Gordon W. Prange, *December 7, 1941: The Day the Japanese Attacked Pearl Harbor*, p. 323.

26. Naval Historical Center, War diary of VJ-1.

27. Army Pearl Harbor Board, Part 29, pp. 2109–2115.

28. Ibid., Part 27, pp. 261–263.

29. Joint Congressional Committee, Part 7, pp. 3191–3192.

30. Roberts Commission, Part 22, p. 50.

31. Joint Congressional Committee, Part 7, p. 3037.

32. Roberts Commission, Part 22, p. 113.

Chapter 11

Seeking the Truth

Japan's ambitions to build an empire and its lack of natural resources created an inevitable longing for the riches of Southeast Asia. Because of those intensions, President Roosevelt focused his international strategy on that country despite the war in Europe. Washington was preparing for a two-ocean war while its citizens were devoted to isolationism. Few in the U.S. government and military believed that war could be avoided. Only the time and place were in doubt.

The Japanese aircraft carrier strike against Oahu on 7 December 1941 was characterized as a surprise or "sneak" attack. However, it only validated what war planners had anticipated for more than a decade. Planning strategy, which had defined the rescue of the Philippines and the decisive fleet engagement, had dictated a vigilant defense for the vital citadel of Oahu. The possibility of a surprise Japanese carrier strike on Oahu was military doctrine. And at the critical juncture in Pacific military history, Oahu's air defense had been hobbled.

Beginning 22 December 1941, the first investigative hearing into the Pearl Harbor disaster began in Honolulu. The Roberts Commission was first and was followed by seven more government inquiries that often overlapped and repeated the work of prior groups. A final joint congressional committee completed the task on 31 May 1946. Kimmel and Short were allowed to present statements and testify at four of the investigations: Roberts Commission, Army Pearl Harbor Board, Navy Court of Inquiry, and the joint congressional committee hearing. The proceedings and exhibits of the combined investigations filled 40 volumes (see Appendix C).

Some of the hearings were grinding, wandering ordeals; others were limited in scope or had special agendas. The earliest probe, the Roberts Commission, was notable for tangential matters peculiar to the chair, Associate Supreme Court Justice Owen J. Roberts. First was the nonissue of sobriety in the Hawaiian military, which the Justice pursued with both military and civilian witnesses. Roberts also was preoccupied with the subject of ground observers. Regardless of all the discussion of Air Warning Service radar, he reduced the matter to an issue of what ground observers might have seen of the approaching attack. Standing on the coast, such observers could not have made a contribution until enemy aircraft were within five miles; therefore, no such system existed. Roberts, along with two other commission members (both retired officers), seemed generally bewildered when it came to understanding modern military technology. Major General Frederick Martin added to the confusion by repeatedly referring to aircraft as "ships."

The Roberts Commission inquiry and later probes were hampered by the secrets of the Magic code-breaking process as well as the mystery of radar. Just when questioning might have produced some critical responses, commission members became mired in their own ignorance and failed to get to the heart of the issue. Many military witnesses who wanted to help were handicapped by their orders, having been advised to answer questions directly and not volunteer any additional information.

General courts-martial were not held because they would interfere with the execution of the war. Kimmel and Short felt this was an injustice. They wanted their day in a public tribunal, but there was a war to be won.

Most of the investigations attempted to determine what blame resided in Washington. And indeed, there was ample reason to allot criticism in that direction. However, despite the revisionist theory that President Roosevelt deliberately provoked Japan and the companion theory that those in Washington conspired to keep Japanese intentions a secret, it seems inconceivable that Roosevelt could have risked destruction of the Pacific Fleet in order to rally public support for a war against the Axis. It is even more inconceivable that Washington's military leadership would have been complicit in taking such a risk.

That the attack failed on a strategic level was due only to flawed target selection—battleships rather than fuel storage tanks, ammunition depots, ship repair, and dry dock facilities—and the fact that the Japanese task force commander, Vice Admiral Chuichi Nagumo, failed to authorize a third wave of attackers.

On analysis, the Washington military establishment does not come off well. It is self-evident from vast Magic intercepts and other diplomatic communications through allies that a war was coming and soon. All of that intelligence was not furnished to the top Hawaiian commanders, due partly to the determination to protect the secret of Magic by limiting dissemination. Extraordinary personality conflicts within the navy between communications and intelligence officers were also at work. Late in 1940, Admiral Stark appointed Rear Admiral Richmond K. Turner to the job of director of war plans. "Terrible Turner," as he was widely known, was a man with an abrasive nature and who was certain of his own judgments. He captured both the intelligence and communications activities and then dispensed them at his whim, to the detriment of Admiral Kimmel's complete enlightenment. [1]

The famous final 14th part of the Japanese diplomatic ultimatum of 7 December 1941, which spelled the end of negotiations and a virtual declaration of war, was received and, after a period of dithering by Washington officials, finally transmitted to Hawaii by an army communications officer who was conducting business as usual with a national crisis at hand. It arrived after the attack had begun. General Marshall should have ensured that the final warning of 7 December was relayed to Short expeditiously.

But even before that, Marshall should have questioned General Short's response to the "war warning" of 27 November. It indicated that Short did not comprehend the gravity of the international situation and the implied threat to his command. Short's judgment also seemed to have been impaired by his obsession with the potential for sabotage from the population of Japanese decent. In his testimony before the Roberts Commission, he even went so far as to make the outrageous charge that some of the 1,500 Japanese-Americans serving in the Hawaiian militia might have fed radar operating schedules to the enemy. There was never a shred of evidence to support such an allegation.[2] General Short's attitude toward those of Japanese ancestry was shared by General Martin who, in his 1944 testimony, still maintained that Hawaii had a very "explosive" population mix. [3]

Short and Martin's bias ignored the fact that there had been no verifiable cases of sabotage among the civil population. In the wake of the attack, Oahu's Japanese community was notable for volunteering blood donations. [4] Subsequently, young men of Japanese ancestry joined the U.S. Army in such record numbers that they formed an independent brigade that served in Italy and became one of the most decorated infantry units of World War II.

The theories concerning a Washington-based conspiracy are, however, largely nullified by the fact that Marshall supplied Short with the latest state-of-the-art radar network, 148 interceptors for air defense, and the Aircraft Warning Service to digest radar data, coordinate information, and then orchestrate a defense. Washington officials were in no way responsible for the delays and lack of cooperation that characterized the employment of the AWS. To the contrary, Marshall had urged the army's Hawaiian Department to get the air defense system improved and functioning. [5]

As the Roberts Commission began its work in Honolulu just 15 days after the attack, Admiral Kimmel and General Short were sacked and replaced. The manner of their relief, the lack of due process afforded them under the Uniform Code of Military Justice, and their reduction in rank have served to convince their proponents of the existence of a high-level plot. Kimmel and Short were "scapegoats" for their superiors, goes the argument. Kimmel-Short advocates also point to the failure of General Douglas MacArthur to prepare for and counter the subsequent Japanese attack in the Philippines. There is ample historic evidence that MacArthur, too, was hesitant, even derelict in his duty. But the Philippines were invaded on 10 December 1941. Washington officials could not even manage to come to its relief, much less implement the offensive naval strategy seeking an encounter with the Imperial Japanese Navy. How could the commanding general of the U.S. Army Forces in the Far East be relieved in the face of the enemy assault? However, MacArthur's mistakes could not nullify the sins of commission and omission of the Hawaiian commanders. Whatever failings were attributable to those in Washington, the commanders in Hawaii had a clear and unmistakable responsibility to protect the base at Pearl Harbor and the Pacific Fleet.

Admiral Kimmel had a primary duty to focus on the various naval scenarios of War Plan Rainbow. But because of his shortage of ships, tankers, and fuel reserves, he believed that the Pacific Fleet was tethered to Pearl Harbor by a long leash, making the tasks of the war plan impossible to attain. [6]

Kimmel implied that a myriad of fleet considerations trumped any responsibility that he had for devoting time to concern over the defense of Pearl Harbor. It was, he pointed out repeatedly, an army assignment in which the navy only participated through Rear Admiral Bloch's 14th Naval District. Yet Kimmel's standing orders to the fleet, 2CL-41, were predicated on the possibility of a surprise air-submarine attack on Oahu by Japan. His orders to the fleet of 14 October 1941 stated in part that "a declaration of war may be preceded by 1) a surprise attack on ships in Pearl Harbor; 2) a surprise submarine attack on ships in operating area; or 3) a combination of these two." [7]

Like much of the Hawaiian naval establishment, Bloch was serenely oblivious to the approaching crisis. He asserted that the Joint Coastal Frontier Defense Plan, in which he was a participant, was not formally operative until M-Day, and the commander in chief (Kimmel) had never declared an emergency. Even the Washington warning 10 days prior to the attack failed to alarm Bloch. The term "war warning" was not, he said, "navy phraseology," and subsequent warning dispatches did nothing to cause him anxiety for the fortress of Oahu. He expressed this lack of concern regarding surprise air attack, even though he felt that the army defenses were deficient in antiaircraft artillery and fighters. [8]

As to the Army Aircraft Warning Service, both Kimmel and Bloch insisted that they had cooperated by providing Curts and Burr for committee meetings and sending Taylor on detached service to the AWS. Kimmel, despite his lack of direct knowledge, felt a certain confidence in the AWS. And because of various drills, he "thought that the radar warning was in very good shape." He went on: "I knew that my staff had taken a very effective part in urging the [14th Naval] District and the army to do certain things in connection with it [the AWS]." Yet Kimmel said that he "did not think it necessary" for a naval officer to be present in the IC. [9]

When shown the Army Air Forces operating manual for the Aircraft Warning Service and its direct reference to the role of navy liaison watch officers at the information center, which was "to identify naval aircraft so as to distinguish them from the enemy," Admiral Kimmel had to admit that he had not seen the document and did not know how the process worked. By way of excusing this oversight, he told the Roberts Commission:

> However much I should have personally checked into this thing—and God knows I wish I had—I had a great many other things to do, and whether the navy liaison officer was present at the radar at the time was something that the officer responsible for the running of the radar should have, it seems to me, looked into. [10]

The quote above reflects Kimmel's lack of knowledge regarding the location of radar sets vis-à-vis the information center at Fort Shafter. And apparently the "officer responsible" must be one of the senior staff at the Aircraft Warning Service who had begged in vain for navy cooperation. In a later inquiry Bloch, as in much of his testimony, continued to be muddled, saying that he had little real knowledge of the AWS, which he thought was in the "development stage" on 7 December 1941 and could not remember any joint air raid drills being conducted. [11]

In his 1955 autobiography *Admiral Kimmel's Story*, Kimmel implied that he was conditioned by a dozen intelligence dispatches received between January and November 1941, all of which "can best be described as 'war warnings.'" [12]

Although seeming somewhat depressed at the Roberts Commission hearings in late December 1941, Kimmel was in high dudgeon by the time of his 1955 autobiography, steadfastly contending that he should be excused from any responsibility for the surprise attack of 7 December 1941 because of a lack of suitable notification from Washington. He insisted this despite the record of:

1. A deteriorating state of international affairs.
2. A war warning.
3. The loss by his own intelligence of two Japanese carrier divisions.
4. Knowledge that there was no distant reconnaiasance from Oahu.

In his autobiography, Kimmel took comfort in the fact that the 1944 Navy Court of Inquiry had exonerated him from any blame for lack of distant reconnaissance on 7 December 1941. He wrote that he had conducted such operations on Monday, 1 December through Thursday, 4 December and then rested his patrol squadrons. He took this action, he said, in order to prepare for what he assumed was a coming war. [13]

The second navy inquiry—The Hewitt Inquiry—only found that Admiral Kimmel had committed errors in judgment inappropriate in a high-ranking navy officer. Admiral Ernest J. King concluded that "no naval officer was at fault to a degree likely to result in conviction if brought to trial, nevertheless the navy cannot evade a share of responsibility for the Pearl Harbor incident." [14]

However, King concluded:

The derelictions on the part of Admiral Stark and Admiral Kimmel were faults of omission rather than faults of commission. In the case in question, they indicate lack of superior judgment necessary for exercising command commensurate with their rank and their assigned duties, rather than culpable inefficiency. [15]

1. Edwin T. Layton, *And I Was There*, pp. 97–102.
2. Roberts Commission, Part 22, p. 102.
3. Army Pearl Harbor Board, Part 28, p. 990.
4. Blake Clark, *Remember Pearl Harbor*, pp. 177–189.
5. Ibid., Exhibit 53, pp. 1605, 1609, 1,625.
6. Husband E. Kimmel, *Admiral Kimmel's Story*, pp. 23–28.
7. Ibid. pp. 189-190.
8. Army Pearl Harbor Board, Part 27, pp. 774–791.
9. Roberts Commission, Part 22, pp. 404–408.
10. Ibid., p. 408.
11. Hart Inquiry, Part 26, pp. 20–29.
12. Husband E. Kimmel, *Admiral Kimmel's Story*, p. 32.
13. Ibid., pp. 65–71.
14. Joint Congressional Committee, Part 39, pp. 398-399.
15. Ibid., p. 400.

Chapter 12

Accountability

The Navy Court of Inquiry exonerated Kimmel, severely censured Stark, and also pointed the finger of blame at the army. A followup navy review, the inquiry by Admiral W. Kent Hewitt, included Kimmel among those responsible. The Army Pearl Harbor Board reciprocated by blaming the navy while also questioning the judgment of General Marshall and other highly placed Washington officers. All of the investigations targeted Short, but none of these 1940s-era probes recognized the depth of his failure to perform his ultimate mission, which was the defense of the Pacific Fleet at Pearl Harbor.

Had Kimmel and Short heeded the warning, many warships could have put to sea, avoiding damage or destruction, and alerted defenses could have ambushed the Japanese carrier air groups. Such a response would have mitigated against losses of vessels, aircraft, and lives, and still had the desired effect of rallying America to a righteous war effort.

Short's first mistake, one that Washington did not correct, was to cancel the alert against outside force and go to Alert No. 1, anti-sabotage. He justified this in his own mind because:

1. He feared sabotage more than an air raid.

2. He had no information to indicate the threat of an air attack.

3. Alerts 2 and 3 against air and naval attack interfered with training. [1]

Short further sought to validate his bad decision by playing the "Philippine training" card:

> Everything indicated to me that the war depart-
> ment did not believe that there was going to be any-
> thing more than sabotage; and, as I have explained, we
> had a very serious training proposition with the Air
> Corps particularly, that if we went into Alert No. 2 or
> 3 instead of No. 1 at the time, that we couldn't meet
> the requirements of the Philippine ferrying business. [2]

Indeed, Rudolph's bomber wing was training pilots to ferry B-17s across the Pacific to the Philippine Air Force. However, that activity was exclusive of the air defense role of the 14th Pursuit Wing. Panelists on the various investigative bodies were sufficiently confused by this waltz through the maze of alerts that they never questioned why the training of bomber crews to ferry B-17s to the Philippines meant that fighter crews on Oahu could not be standing on alert against a possible air attack. The fighter crews were not training for anything after noon on Saturday, 6 December, having been allowed the weekend off.

Short's mindset that the Japanese fleet posed no real threat to Oahu, that the population was a grave menace, and that thinking otherwise would interfere with training is the height of faulty reasoning. One has to wonder why no investigative body ever called on him to explain why during a war alert he could not have the Aircraft Warning

Service fully prepared and manned for a No. 1 sabotage alert with fighters at Wheeler ready to defend in the event of an air raid alert.

As for distant search, Short shrugged off any responsibility. He assumed that the navy was taking care of such operations, although he never inquired about such navy activity during any of his many face-to-face meetings with Kimmel. Despite this absence of knowledge, he advised Marshall that he had a "liaison with the navy." [3]

The members of the navy hierarchy, despite insistence that they were cooperating, had dealt the Aircraft Warning Service a fatal blow by not participating in the day-to-day operation of the information center. However, air raid defense was the responsibility of Short, whose primary mission was the protection of Oahu, and he was its chief saboteur.

The charges leveled against General Short by the army judge advocate were repeated before the joint congressional committee hearings in 1946. Short was equivocal before the Roberts Commission, just days after the attack; however, he became selective in his recall and was in full denial at the congressional hearings four years later:

CHARGE NO. 1: FAILURE TO PROVIDE AN ADEQUATE INSHORE AERIAL PATROL.

Short responded, "Not guilty." He claimed that he had an adequate 20-mile anti-submarine air patrol with his one observation squadron and the fighter units that periodically flew offshore within sight of Oahu. However, none of them flew at all between noon Saturday, 6 December 1941, and the time of the Japanese attack Sunday morning, 7 December. It was during the early hours Sunday morning that Japanese midget submarines approached Oahu. At least one entered Pearl Harbor, and one was detected and sunk by the destroyer *Ward*. Another was attacked just after the air raid began by the destroyer *Monaghan* as she sortied from Pearl

Harbor. This midget submarine, its steering damaged, eventually grounded off Bellows Field. The Hawaiian Air Force played no part in this activity despite many assertions regarding its anti-submarine capability. [4]

CHARGE NO. 2: FAILURE TO PROVIDE ADEQUATE ANTIAIRCRAFT DEFENSE.

Short responded, "Not guilty." He said he would have had an adequate antiaircraft defense if only the war department had given him information of an imminent air attack, meaning the unsuitability of the 27 November 1941 war warning from his viewpoint. [5]

CHARGE NO. 3: FAILURE TO SET UP AN INTERCEPTOR COMMAND.

Again, Short responded, "Not guilty," adding, "We were training personnel as fast as we could to operate an effective interceptor command, and it was set up and operating as effectively as it could." [6]

The 14th Pursuit Wing, the air arm of the Interceptor Command, was not a new organization. The so-called interceptor command was to be established when the department signal officer got out of the way and turned his radar and information center personnel over to General Davidson. That was to have taken place just days before the attack, but as with so many matters on Short's agenda, it just drifted. In any event, the fighter aircraft and pilots of the 14th Pursuit Wing were dismissed from all flight operations after a Saturday review. No units were standing alert.

CHARGE NO. 4: FAILURE TO PROVIDE A PROPER AIRCRAFT WARNING SERVICE.

"Not guilty," said Short. "We were training our personnel as fast as we could to set up an effective Aircraft Warning Service. It was in operation." [7]

It was when speaking of the AWS, before any investigative body, that General Short repeatedly demonstrated his ignorance. The initial test of the service had occurred on 27 September 1941. Immediately thereafter Short wrote to General Marshall that the system would be "operational within 30 days." He told the Roberts Commission that it was operational around 1 November. Even as late as the 1946 joint congressional committee hearings, he could not seem to realize that the running of the radar equipment and the mere presence of a few personnel in the information center did not constitute a fully manned and completely functional system.

General Short did not sanction navy obstruction regarding the lack of staffing at the information center, but he did nothing to correct the problem. begging the assumption that he did not understand the need.

CHARGE NO. 5: FAILURE TO PROVIDE FOR THE TRANSMISSION OF APPROPRIATE WARNINGS TO INTERESTED AGENCIES.

General Short responded that the war warning from General Marshall had restricted him "by direct order" from transmitting the warning to anyone but essential officers. Short said that if he had disseminated the warning to everybody at the AWS, "we would have had to give it to all the enlisted men." [8]

While technically correct, this is a ludicrous reason for not advising key air force officers below General Martin's rank that war was about to break out and vigilance was in order. Davidson, Tindal, Bergquist, Taylor, and Tetley were all in the dark as to Short's war warning and his intentions, and it was they who could have been watchful for a surprise air attack while the commander in chief worried about guarding bridges and public utilities from sabotage.

CHARGE NO. 6: FAILURE TO ESTABLISH A PROPER SYSTEM OF DEFENSE COOPERATION AND COORDINATION WITH THE NAVY.

General Short again pleaded, "Not guilty. We had full and complete plans for the defense by cooperation with the navy, which had been approved by General Marshall and Admiral Stark." [9]

The cooperation between the various branches of each service, and between the army and navy in Hawaii, was spoken of with almost religious fervor by ranking officers during their post-attack testimony. For the army's part it had been urged by General Marshall just after Short took command of the army's Hawaiian Department. But real cooperation was a charade, performed in a sociable manner with the greatest cordiality. The military officials would meet on matters of defense, professing their belief in joint planning and coordinated operations. Yet, in ways that ultimately tore the fabric of Oahu's protection, there was subtle resistance to joint partnership. It was like a bad marriage, where each took the vows regarding mutual trust but silently determined to follow their own maxims.

The facade of cooperation was displayed in a variety of boards and committees that considered, among other things, joint maneuvers, new airfields, communications, air traffic routes, aircraft operating areas, and aircraft recognition. On the significant issues of command and control, however, senior Hawaiian commanders resisted allowing the other service to dictate matters. This is best demonstrated by an exchange of correspondence that began on 15 October 1941 with a cable from Admiral Stark, the chief of naval operations, to Admirals Kimmel, Bloch, and Bellinger. Stark urged that consideration be given to a "combined operating center" for both the navy and the army in Hawaii. The navy chiefs, along with General Short, suggested a variety of reasons why such a facility was inappropriate for their various arms. The correspondence with multiple endorsements continued back and forth between Oahu and Washington right up to the time of the attack, after which Washington ordered the establishment of such a center. A post-attack memorandum by an officer in the chief of naval operation's office, commenting on the stubbornness emanating from Oahu, noted: "The commandant, Fourteenth Naval District, commanding general Hawaiian Department, and the commander in chief, Pacific Fleet, have entirely missed the boat." [10]

Within a week of the attack and as a consequence of the dual command failure, military leaders meeting with the president established the first unified commands: On 17 December 1941, the command of all U.S. military forces in the Hawaii area was placed under the commander in chief of the Pacific Fleet, Admiral Chester W. Nimitz (Kimmel's replacement), and those in the Panama area under the commander in chief in Panama and later the Caribbean area, Lieutenant General Frank Andrews. Ultimately the Southwest Pacific Command was created under General Douglas MacArthur. These joint regional commands and those later established in other combat zones functioned until the final victory in 1945.

CHARGE NO. 7: FAILURE TO ISSUE ADEQUATE ORDERS TO HIS SUBORDINATES AS TO THEIR DUTIES IN CASE OF SUDDEN ATTACK.

General Short pleaded, "Not guilty." He claimed that he could not advise his subordinates in such a matter because the War Department had limited dissemination and had not told him to expect a sudden hostile attack. [11]

Here again Short makes the illogical assertion that warning his air defense of possible enemy action would violate his orders. During prior weeks when the 14th Pursuit Wing had been on alert with pilots in the cockpits and ground crews standing by, the purpose of the exercise was to prepare for a hostile air attack that might be imminent. Short's order of a weekend stand-down implied that the risk had vanished, fostering confusion among the pursuit squadrons.

CHARGE NO. 8: FAILURE TO TAKE ADEQUATE MEASURES TO PROTECT THE FLEET AND NAVAL BASE AT PEARL HARBOR.

Again General Short argued that he had done what he claimed Marshall had ordered, protecting Oahu from sabotage. [12]

From the time of his briefing before assuming command of the army's Hawaiian Department, General Short was well aware that a surprise attack from Japanese air and naval forces posed the primary threat to his command. Marshall's warning made a point of stating that he should not "jeopardize" his defense.

CHARGE NO. 9: FAILURE TO HAVE HIS AIRPLANES DISPERSED IN ANTICIPATION OF A HOSTILE ATTACK, AFTER HAVING BEEN WARNED OF THE DANGER THEREOF.

General Short said, "Not guilty." It was the War Department's fault, he claimed, following his theme that the war warning of impending hostile action did not specify air attack. [13]

His focus on the theme of sabotage can at best be considered a monumental error in judgment.

CHARGE NO. 10: FAILURE TO HAVE HIS AIRPLANES IN A STATE OF READINESS FOR AN ATTACK.

Once again, Short claimed that he was not at fault because he thought that the War Department war warning compelled him to go on a sabotage alert. Thus his combat aircraft were on four-hour notice. [14]

During alert No. 1, ammunition and in some cases guns were removed from aircraft, the same ones that had been armed 10 days before. No members of any investigative panel thought to ask why he did not have one squadron on air raid standby, armed, fueled, crewed, and prepared to scramble, as long as they were on the hangar line, being guarded day and night.

In earlier testimony before the joint congressional committee, Short admitted that his fighters could not have scrambled when the radar stations first reported the contact that turned out to be the Japanese first wave. But he said there would have been time to disperse the aircraft to bunkers. [15]

At that point in time, it would have taken several hundred airmen in near proximity to push the fighters from the ramp to the bunkers. There were only a limited number of tugs for such an exercise. And Wheeler Field's enlisted personnel were scattered in mess halls, barracks, and off base on passes on Sunday morning, all in response to General Short's stand-down.

CHARGE NO. 11: FAILURE TO PROVIDE FOR THE PROTECTION OF MILITARY PERSONNEL, THEIR FAMILIES, ETC., AND OF CIVILIAN EMPLOYEES ON VARIOUS RESERVATIONS.

This was not a worthy charge. No funding had been provided to squirrel away both military and civilian populations in the event of a surprise air attack. Most of the civilian dead were not the victims of the Japanese but rather army and navy antiaircraft fire falling back on populated areas.

One of the most remarkable omissions of command by General Short, the failure to conduct reconnaissance as ordered in the 27 November war warning, was dismissed by various investigating panels that accepted the claim by Martin, and repeated by Short, Kimmel, and Bellinger, that the Hawaiian Air Force had only six B-17Ds suitable for such operations. This claim was declared over and over until it became dogma, the big lie that the army could not be blamed for not following orders to search, since it had not been given the force of 180 B-17s that Martin had pined for.

Short even embellished on Martin's prior fraudulent assertions about the force of Douglas B-18s before the joint congressional committee. In further denouncing the unsuitability of the B-18s, Short said that they only had a "maximum speed of 150 miles per hour." The top speed of the aircraft was 217 miles per hour, and it cruised at 167. [16] Because the various investigative panels accepted that these and other Air Force aircraft were nonexistent or useless for reconnaissance, they never asked any embarrassing questions about why the army did not arrange some sort of joint distant search program with the navy, which had also claimed that it had limited resources.

The two top commanders in Hawaii were not solely responsible for the failures that led to 7 December 1941. Apart from Washington's sins, noted in the findings of several investigations, there was clear failure among the staffs of Kimmel and Short. Kimmel said more than once that he could not be everywhere. True though that may be, the failure of a staff officer reflects on the stewardship of the commander. It is the leader who is charged with ultimate responsibility and stands accountable.

In 1995 the Department of Defense conducted yet another review of the Pearl Harbor matter for the sole purpose of ascertaining whether the dismissal and "demotion" of Kimmel and Short were excessively harsh. That extensive study, chaired by Under Secretary of Defense Edwin Dorn, concluded that responsibility for the disaster should be broadly shared with Washington. However, Dorn concluded that Kimmel and Short could not be absolved of their accountability as the on-scene commanders who had failed to employ the resources available to maintain a higher level of vigilance and defense. In the report Dorn wrote:

> I cannot conclude that Admiral Kimmel and
> General Short were victims of unfair official actions

and thus I cannot conclude that the official remedy
of advancement on the retirement list [is] in order.
Admiral Kimmel and General Short did not have all
the resources they felt necessary. Had they been provided more intelligence and earlier guidance they
might have understood their situation more clearly
and behaved differently. But this is not a basis for
contradicting the conclusions, drawn consistently
over several investigations, that Admiral Kimmel
and General Short committed errors of judgment.
As commanders, they were accountable. Admiral
Kimmel and General Short suffered greatly for Pearl
Harbor. They lost men for whom they were responsible. They felt that too much blame was placed on
them. Their children and grandchildren continue to
be haunted by it all. For all this, there can be sadness.
But there can be no official remedy. [17]

In May 1999, the U.S. Congress passed a "sense of the
Congress" resolution seeking to reinstate the ranks of Kimmel and
Short. Legislators undertook this action without any further investigation. The resolution was appended to a National Defense
Authorization Bill and was signed by President Bill Clinton but did
not require any action by the Department of Defense. Senate supporters invoked the well-worn theory that the Hawaiian commanders were scapegoats. Senator Strom Thurmond, a South Carolina
Republican, called Admiral Kimmel and General Short the last two
victims of Pearl Harbor. Truth continues to be the ultimate and
enduring casualty.

One is left to ponder how history might have been altered—lives
saved, the war shortened—had Kimmel and Short cooperated fully

and employed the defense resources at hand. In postwar interviews, two of the Aircraft Warning Service pioneers reflected on the failure:

Ken Bergquist: A few of us Indians really tried to get the system in operation in time despite the man-made obstacles. We almost made it.

Bill Taylor: The P-36 and the P-40 were inferior to the Japanese Zero in some respects, but in greater numbers than the few that got up, they would have caused chaos among the slow-flying Japanese bombers, the torpedo-carrying Kates in particular. Certainly this would have mitigated the damage caused to our ships.

There is no question among the surviving flyers of the Hawaiian Air Force about the outcome of the air battle of 7 December 1941 had they been alerted and permitted to engage the enemy in greater numbers. Norval Heath, a lieutenant and fighter pilot at Wheeler Field on that day, insists, "We would have given a damn good account of ourselves."

1. Roberts Commission, Part 22, p. 36.

2. Army Pearl Harbor Board, Part 27, p. 232.

3. Ibid., pp. 158–165.

4. Joint Congressional Committee, Part 7, p. 3,191 and Roberts Commission and Victor A. Dybdal, "What a Way to Start a War," *Naval History*, December 2001.

5. Joint Congressional Committee, Part 7, pp. 3191-3192.

6. Ibid., p. 3192.

7. Ibid.

8. Ibid.

9. Ibid.

10. Part 17, pp. 2736–2744.

11. Ibid., Part 7, p. 3192.

12. Ibid., p. 3194.

13. Ibid.

14. Ibid.

15. Ibid., p. 2995.

16. Ibid., p. 2962.

17. Edwin Dorn, under secretary of defense, in a letter accompanying report on Advancement of Rear Admiral Kimmel and Major General Short on the retired list, dated 15 December 1995.

Epilogue

President Franklin D. Roosevelt called December 7, 1941 "a date which will live in infamy." It shattered the careers of some Hawaiian-based officers. Two were censured. A few were quietly retired, and others went on to serve with distinction in the war that continued for three and a half years. Briefly, here is what happened in the careers of those who had prominent roles in the Pearl Harbor attack:

Admiral Husband E. Kimmel: He was relieved of his command on 17 December 1941 and placed on inactive duty. He then retired. He was reduced to his prewar rank of rear admiral and died in 1968.

Lieutenant General Walter C. Short: He was relieved of his command on 17 December 1941 and placed on inactive duty and then retired. He was reduced to his prewar rank of major general and died in 1949.

Rear Admiral Claude C. Bloch: He returned to the mainland and retired in 1942. He died in 1967.

Major General Frederick L. Martin: He was relieved of command 18 December 1941 and returned to the mainland as commanding officer of the Second Air Force Central Technical Training Wing at St. Louis, Missouri. He retired because of ill health in 1944 and died in 1954.

Brigadier General Howard C. Davidson: He led the Seventh Fighter Command until June 1942. Then he returned to the United States and was reassigned to India as a commander of the Tenth Air Force. He flew combat missions in C-47 and B-25 aircraft and later was awarded the Distinguished Service Medal, Distinguished Flying Cross, and Purple Heart. He retired in 1946 with rank of major general and died in 1984.

Rear Admiral Patrick N. L. Bellinger: He was reassigned as an air commander of the Atlantic Fleet from August 1942 to February 1946. His decorations included the Navy Cross and he retired in 1947 after attaining rank of vice admiral. He died in 1962.

Brigadier General Jacob H. Rudolph: He returned to the mainland in January 1942 and served as commanding officer of the Spokane Air Depot. He retired 1944 and died in 1954.

Colonel William J. Flood: He performed various 7th Air Force assignments, ending his service as chief of staff of the 7th Air Force in 1945. He attained rank of brigadier general and retired in 1946 and died 1977.

Lieutenant Commander William E. G. Taylor: He returned to the United States March 1942 and served as the officer in charge of Navy night fighting, Project Affirm. In 1945, he was assigned various posts in the Atlantic Fleet and North Africa serving as a commanding officer in Port Lyautey, Morocco. His decorations included the Bronze Star. He retired in 1951 with rank of captain and died in 1992.

Lieutenant Commander Logan C. Ramsey: He was assigned as an operations officer Midway in May through June in 1942. He served as chief of staff to commander aircraft in Pacific Fleet until March 1943 and returned to the United States for reassignment as a commanding officer of the aircraft carrier *Block Island,* which was on an Atlantic anti-submarine mission. In March 1944, he was assigned as chief of staff to the Commander Fleet Air, Norfolk. His decorations included the Legion of Merit with cluster, Bronze Star, and Commendation Medal. He retired 1949 with rank of rear admiral and died in 1972.

Lieutenant Commander Edwin T. Layton: He was the chief of intelligence for CINCPAC throughout World War II. After the war, he established the Navy intelligence school, served as assistant director of intelligence for the joint chiefs of staff, and as the assistant chief of staff to CINCPAC. His decorations included the Distinguished Service Medal and Commendation Medal. He retired in 1959 with rank of rear admiral and died in 1984.

Major Kenneth P. Bergquist: He established air defense system in New Caledonia for Seventh Air Force and served various assignments with Army Air Force headquarters. In 1944, he was the deputy chief of operations for the 73rd Bomb Wing in Saipan and flew B-29 combat missions to Japan. In 1945, he served as deputy commander of the Seventh Fighter Command in Iwo Jima. His decorations included the Distinguished Service Medal, Legion of Merit with two oak leaf clusters, Air Medal, and Bronze Star. He retired in 1965 attaining rank of major general; he died in 1990.

Major Lorry N. Tindal: He continued his service with the Hawaiian 7th Fighter Command until he was reassigned in 1943 to Army Air Force headquarters. As the chief of staff and operations with the Ninth Air Force, he coordinated D-Day operations. He held various assignments at Hickam Field, Hawaii, and in the United States until he retired as colonel in 1959. His decorations included the Legion of Merit with oak leaf cluster and the Commendation Medal with cluster. He died in 1960.

Lieutenant Colonel Carroll A. Powell: He was assigned as signal officer for the Pacific Ocean Area, Fort Shafter, Hawaii. He later attained the rank of brigadier general and died in 1948.

Captain Wilfred H. Tetley: He helped establish the air defense radar system on Niihau, Fiji, and New Caledonia. His final war assignment was with Southeast Asia's Allied Command, serving in its radar intelligence program. After the war, he was assigned to the Air Force Research Center in Cambridge, Massachusetts. His decorations included the Army Commendation Medal. He retired from the army in 1962 with the rank of colonel and died 2002.

First Lieutenant Kermit A. Tyler: He commanded the 44th Fighter Squadron on Guadalcanal and was credited for downing at least one Japanese Zero. He flew 30 combat missions in fighters and later was assigned as a operations officer for the Thirteenth Fighter Command. His decorations included the Legion of Merit and the Air Medal. He returned to United States for various assignments and attained rank of lieutenant colonel at retirement.

Appendix A

PRINCIPALS

The principal individuals discussed in this study, in alphabetical order, along with ranks and duties on 7 December 1941, are as follows:

Navy

Bellinger, Patrick N. L., Rear Admiral, commander
patrol wings, Oahu

Bloch, Claude C., Rear Admiral, commandant 14th Naval
District, Oahu

Burr, Harold S., Lieutenant, naval liaison to army, 14th Naval
District, Oahu

Curts, Maurice E., Captain, communications officer,
Pacific Fleet, Oahu

Davis, Arthur C., Captain, aviation officer, Pacific Fleet, Oahu

DeLany, Walter S., Captain, operations officer, Pacific Fleet, Oahu

Earle, John B., Captain, chief of staff, 14th Naval District, Oahu

Halsey, William F., Vice Admiral, commanding Task Force 2

Kimmel, Husband E., Admiral, commander in chief, Pacific
Fleet, Oahu

Layton, Edwin T., Lieutenant Commander, intelligence officer,
Pacific Fleet, Oahu

Newton, John H., Rear Admiral, commanding Task Force 3

Ramsey, Logan C., Lieutenant Commander, chief of staff to
commander patrol wings, Oahu

Rochefort, Joseph J., Commander, officer in charge, combat
intelligence unit, Oahu

Smith, William W., Captain, chief of staff, Pacific Fleet, Oahu

Stark, Harold R., Admiral, chief of naval operations,
Washington, D.C.

Taylor, William E. G., Lieutenant Commander, attached Hawaiian
Air Force

Turner, Richmond K., Rear Admiral, navy chief of war plans,
Washington, D.C.

Army

Bergquist, Kenneth P., Major, operations officer, Air Warning
Service, Oahu

Bicknell, George W., Lieutenant Colonel, assistant intelligence
officer, Hawaiian Department

Davidson, Howard C., Brigadier General, commanding 14th
Pursuit Wing, Oahu

Fielder, Kendall J., Colonel, intelligence officer,
Hawaiian Department

Flood, William J., Colonel, commanding Wheeler Field, Oahu

Marshall, George C., General, army chief of staff, Washington, D.C.

Martin, Frederick L., Major General, commanding Hawaiian
Air Force

Murphy, W. H., Lieutenant Colonel, deputy signal officer,
Hawaiian Department

Mollison, James A., Colonel, chief of staff, Hawaiian Air Force

Powell, Carroll A., Lieutenant Colonel, signal officer,
Hawaiian Department

Rudolph, Jacob H., Brigadier General, commanding 18th
Bomb Wing, Oahu

Short, Walter C., Lieutenant General, commanding
Hawaiian Department

Tetley, Wilfred W., Captain, commanding officer of
Signal Company Aircraft Warning Service Hawaii

Tindal, Lorry N., Major, Controller, Aircraft Warning Service, Oahu

Tyler, Kermit A., First Lieutenant, 78th Pursuit Squadron, Oahu

Appendix B

PEARL HARBOR AIR RAID DRILLS

Following are the dates on which Pearl Harbor air raid drills were held:

24–25 March 1941*

24 April 1941

12 May 1941, joint exercises

13 May 1941

19 June 1941

10 July 1941

26 July 1941

1 August 1941

20 August 1941

5 September 1941

27 September 1941, joint exercises, *Enterprise* air group as enemy attacker.

13 October 1941, joint exercises

27 October 1941, joint exercises

10 November 1941, alert drill

12 November 1941, joint exercises

Sources:

* Hq 14th Pursuit Wing, ops order 14, 20 March 1941

All other dates: Roberts Commission Exhibits, Part 24, pp. 1397-98, 1424, 1934-35

Appendix C

PEARL HARBOR ATTACK INVESTIGATIONS

There were multiple, sometimes overlapping investigations into the Pearl Harbor attack. This is a list of the various government hearings in chronological order. "Part" notations in the footnotes refer to the numbered volumes of the collected proceedings published by the Government Printing Office. All of the material was used in this study.

Roberts Commission, 18 December 1941 to 23 January 1942, Parts 22–25

Hart Inquiry, 12 February 1944 to 15 June 1944, Part 26

Army Pearl Harbor Board, 20 July 1944 to 20 October 1944, Parts 27–31

Navy Court of Inquiry, 24 July 1944 to 19 October 1944, Parts 32–33

Clarke Investigation, 14 September 1944 to 4 August 1945, Part 34

Clausen Investigation, 23 November 1944 to 12 September 1945, Part 35

Hewitt Inquiry, 14 May 1945 to 11 July 1945, Part 36–38

Joint Congressional Committee on the Investigation of the Pearl Harbor Attack, 15 November 1945 to 31 May 1946, Parts 1–21, Part 39, and one unnumbered final volume

Appendix D

U.S. NAVY AIRCRAFT IN HAWAIIAN ISLANDS, 7 DECEMBER 1941

UNIT (1)	TYPE	LOCATION	NOTES
Patrol Squadrons			
VP-11	12 PBY-5	Kaneohe	
VP-12	12 PBY-5	Kaneohe	one under repair
VP-14	9 PBY-5	Kaneohe	two under repair
	3 PBY-5	airborne	Pearl Harbor approaches
VP-21	1 PBY-3	Ford Island	under repair; 11 PBY operating from Midway
VP-22	12 PBY-3	Ford Island	two under repair
VP-23	12 PBY-5	Ford Island	one under repair
VP-24	2 PBY-5	Ford Island	
	4 PBY-5	airborne	Lahina Roads

Utility planes

VJ-1	9 J2F-4	Ford Island	utility floatplane
	11 JRS-1	Ford Island	cargo flying boat
VJ-2	10 J2F-4	Ford Island	utility floatplane
	2 PBY-1	Ford Island	
VJ-3	2 BT-1	Maui	dive bomber
	4 JRB-1	Maui	utility transport
	2 JRF-4	Maui	utility floatplane
	1 J2F-4	Maui	

Battleships and cruisers (some aircraft ashore)

(Two)	28 OS2U	floatplanes
	28 SOC/SON	floatplanes

Seaplane tenders

	5 OS2U	floatplanes

Miscellaneous and command aircraft

7 F2A-3	Ford Island	Storage, awaiting assignment
4 F4F-3	Ford Island	Left by carrier air groups
3 SBD-2	Ford Island	Left by carrier air groups
7 TBD-1	Ford Island	Left by carrier air groups
1 OS2U	Kaneohe	

Note 1: See glossary for navy-marine squadron abbreviations.

Note 2: These scouting float aircraft were assigned to cruisers and battleships in harbor. Some were still aboard their ships while most others were at Ford Island Naval Air Station.

Source: Naval Historical Center, Washington, D.C., monthly status of naval aircraft, 30 November, 1941.

Appendix E

U.S. MARINE CORPS AIRCRAFT
IN HAWAIIAN ISLANDS, 7 DECEMBER 1941

VMF-211	10 F4F-3	Ewa	11 additional on Wake Island
	1 SNJ-3	Ewa	trainer
VMSB-231	5 SB2U-1	Ewa	Plus 7 listed as spares
			(used for spare parts),
			18 additional on carrier
			Lexington en route
			to Midway
VMSB-232	19 SBD-1	Ewa	
	3 SBD-2	Ewa	
VMJ-252	2 J2F-4	Ewa	
	1 JRS-1	Ewa	Amphibian transport
	1 JO-2	Ewa	Utility transport
	2 R3D-2	Ewa	Transport DC-2

| 1 SBD-1 | Ewa |
| 1 SB2U-1 | Ewa |

Sources: Naval Historical Center, Washington, D.C., monthly status of naval aircraft, 30 November 30, 1941, and *History of Marine Corps Aviation in WW II*, Robert Sherrod, 1952.

Appendix F

U.S. ARMY AIR FORCES AIRCRAFT ON OAHU, 7 DECEMBER 1941

TYPE	ON HAND	OPERABLE	DESTROYED	AVAILABLE POST-ATTACK
A-12A	2	2	—	1
A-20A	12	5	2	9
AT-6	4	3	1	2
B-12A	3	1	—	1
B-17D(1)	12	6	5	4
B-18	33	2	12	11
B-24A(2)	1	1	1	—
C-33	2	2	—	2

OA-8	1	1	—	1
OA-9	3	3	2	1
O-47B	7	5	—	5
O-49	2	2	1	1
P-26A	8	7	5	2
P-26B	6	3	1	2
P-36A	39	20	4	16
P-40B	87	55	37	25
P-40C	12	9	5	2
Totals	234	146	76	83

Note 1: The 12 B-17C and E aircraft that arrived during the Japanese air attack are not listed above. One was destroyed, one was severely damaged, and one that landed at Kahuku could not be repaired and flown for one week; some of the remaining B-17s sustained minor damage but nine were available within 24 hours.

Note 2: The single long-range Consolidated B-24A Liberator had arrived on 5 December from the Middle East. It was unarmed and being outfitted with machine guns at Hickam Field. It was then destined to be transferred to the Philippine Air Force for photo reconnaissance tasks over the Japanese Mandated Islands. It was destroyed at Hickam by Japanese bombs.

Source: Office of Air Force History, *Operational History of the Seventh Air Force, 7 December 1941 to 6 November 1943.*

Appendix G

JAPANESE CARRIER AIRCRAFT USED IN OAHU ATTACK

First wave led by Commander Mitsuo Fuchida

	A6M2 Zero fighters	D3A1 Val dive bombers	B5N2 Kate horizontal bombers	B5N2 Kate torpedo bombers	Total
Akagi	9	—	15	12	36
Kaga	9	—	14	12	35
Soryu	8	—	10	8	26
Hiryu	6	—	10	8	24

Shokaku	6	26	—	—	32
Zuikaku	5	25	—	—	30
Total					183

Second wave led by Lieutenant Commander Shigekazu Shimazak

Akagi	9	18	—	—	27
Kaga	9	26	—	—	35
Soryu	9	17	—	—	26
Hiryu	8	17	—	—	25
Shokaku	—	—	27	—	27
Zuikaku	—	—	27	—	27
Total					171

Note: A total of 39 A6M2 fighters were retained aboard the carriers to conduct combat air patrols and did not take part in the attack. One Zero lost power on takeoff and ditched. The pilot was rescued by a Japanese destroyer.

JAPANESE COMBAT LOSSES

Nine Zeros, 15 Vals, and five Kates with 55 air crewmembers. Another 19 aircraft were jettisoned after their return to their carriers because of battle damage.

Appendix H

OVERALL U. S. LOSSES FROM JAPANESE ATTACK OF 7 DECEMBER 1941

NAVY SHIPS

Battleships

Arizona BB-39 — Sunk at berth with heavy loss of life. Never raised.

California BB-44 — Sunk at berth with moderate loss of life. Raised, repaired, and saw service again.

Maryland BB-46 — Damaged and repaired.

Nevada BB-36 — Heavily damaged and beached. Repaired and saw service again.

Oklahoma BB-37 — Sunk and capsized at berth with heavy loss of life. Raised but never saw service again.

Pennsylvania BB-38 — Minor bomb damage. Repaired and saw service again.

Tennessee BB-43	Moderate bomb damage. Repaired and saw sevice again.
West Virginia BB-48	Sunk at berth with moderate loss of life. Raised, repaired, and saw service again.

Light Cruisers

Helena CL-50	Moderate damage. Repaired and saw service again.
Honolulu CL-48	Light damage. Repaired and saw service again.
Raleigh CL-7	Moderate damage. Repaired and saw service again.

Destroyers

Cassin DD-372	Destroyed in dry dock. Rebuilt and saw service again.
Downes DD-375	Destroyed in dry dock. Rebuilt and saw service again.
Shaw DD-373	Destroyed in dry dock. Rebuilt and saw service again.

Other ships

Utah AG-16 (ex-BB target ship)	Sunk and capsized. Never repaired.
Curtiss AV-4 (Seaplane tender)	Light damage repaired.
Oglala ARG-31 (Mine layer)	Sunk. Raised and repaired.
Vestal AR-4 (Repair ship)	Beached. Repaired.

AIRCRAFT

U.S. NAVY	92 destroyed	31 damaged
ARMY AIR FORCE	77 destroyed	77 damaged

CASUALTIES

	Killed or Died of Wounds	Wounded
U.S. NAVY	2,008	710
MARINE CORPS	109	69
U.S. ARMY	218	364
CIVILIANS	68	35
Total	2,403	1,178

Appendix I

SOURCES OF INFORMATION

We are indebted to many individuals for their assistance in providing firsthand information and historic data for this work. All were interviewed in person or through correspondence. Various organizations and documentary sources also provided assistance. Those who contributed are listed below:

Individuals

Abe, Yasujiro, Petty Officer, Imperial Japanese Navy

Abe, Zenji, Lieutenant, Imperial Japanese Navy

Ahola, Tuevo E., Colonel, United States Air Force

Beckwith, James O., Colonel, United States Air Force

Bergquist, Kenneth P., Major General, United States Air Force

Burt, William R., Lieutenant Colonel, United States Air Force

Davidson, Howard C., Major General, United States Air Force

Heath, Norval K., Colonel, United States Air Force

Michaud, Philippe A., Corporal, Signal Company Aircraft
  Warning Service Hawaii, United States

Mooney, George B., Sergeant, Signal Company Aircraft
Warning Service Hawaii, United States
Okajima, Kiyoguma, Lieutenant, Imperial Japanese Navy
Rasmussen, Philip M., Colonel, United States Air Force
Rogers, Robert J., Colonel, United States Air Force
Sanders, Lewis M., Colonel, United States Air Force
Shiga, Yoshi, Lieutenant, Imperial Japanese Navy
Taylor, Charles, Colonel, United States Air Force
Taylor, Kenneth M., Brigadier General, United States Air Force
Taylor, William E.G., Captain, United States Naval Reserves
Tetley, Wilfred H., Colonel, United States Signal Corps
Thacker, John M., Colonel, United States Air Force
Tyler, Kermit A., Lieutenant Colonel, United States Air Force

Organizations

Hamilton Library, University of Hawaii, Honolulu, Hawaii
National Air & Space Museum, Washington, D.C.
Naval Historical Center, Washington, D.C.
National Archives II, College Park, Maryland
Office of Air Force History, Simpson Historical Research
Agency, Maxwell Air Force Base, Alabama
Japanese National Defense College, Tokyo

Bibliography

Beach, Edward L. 1995. *Scapegoats: A Defense of Kimmel and Short at Pearl Harbor.* Annapolis, Md.: Naval Institute Press.

Beekman, Allan. 1982. *The Niihau Incident.* Honolulu, Hawaii: Heritage Press of the Pacific.

Chenoweth, Candace A., and A. Kam Napier. 1991. *Shuffleboard Pilots: The History of the Women's Air Raid Defense in Hawaii, 1941-1945.* Honolulu, Hawaii: Arizona Memorial Museum Association.

Clark, Blake. 1943. *Remember Pearl Harbor.* New York: Harper & Brothers.

Clausen, Henry C., and Bruce Lee. 1992. *Pearl Harbor Final Judgment.* New York: Crown Publishers.

Cohen, Stan. 1981. *East Wind Rain*. Missoula, Mont.: Pictorial Histories Publishing Company.

79th Congress of the United States. 1946. *Hearings before the Joint Committee on the Investigation of the Pearl Harbor Attack*. 40 vols. Washington: U.S. Government Printing Office.

Craven, Wesley F., and James L. Cate. 1948. *Plans and Early Operations*. Vol. 1 of *The Army Air Forces in World War II*. Chicago: The University of Chicago Press.

Davis, Burke. 1967. *The Billy Mitchell Affair*. New York: Random House.

Department of Defense. 1978. *The Magic Background of Pearl Harbor*. 8 vols. Washington: U.S. Government Printing Office.

Dull, Paul S. 1978. *Battle History of the Imperial Japanese Navy (1941–1945)*. Annapolis, Md.: Naval Institute Press.

Evans, David C., and Raymond O'Connor. 1969. *The Japanese Navy in World War II*. Annapolis, Md.: Naval Institute Press.

Evans, David C., and Mark A. Peattie. 1997. *Kaigun: Strategy, Tactics, and Technology in Imperial Japanese Navy 1887–1941*. Annapolis, Md.: Naval Institute Press.

Farago, Ladislas. 1966. *The Broken Seal*. New York: Random House.

Fuchida, Mitsuo, and Masatake Okumiya. 1955. *Midway, The Battle That Doomed Japan*. Annapolis, Md.: Naval Institute Press.

Fuchida, Mitsuo. 1952. *I Led the Attack on Pearl Harbor*. Annapolis, Md.: Naval Institute Press.

Gannon, Michael. 2001. *Pearl Harbor Betrayed*. New York: Henry Holt and Company.

Hoehling, A. A. 1978. *The Day the Admirals Slept Late*. New York: Kensington Publishing.

Kimmel, Husband E. 1955. *Admiral Kimmel's Story*. Chicago: Henry Regnery Company.

Kuborn, John R., and Leatrice R. Arakaki. 1991. *7 December 1941: The Air Force Story*. Hickam Air Force Base, Hawaii: Pacific Air Forces Office of History.

Lambert, John W. 1990. *The Pineapple Air Force: Pearl Harbor to Tokyo*. St. Paul, Minn.: Phalanx Publishing Company.

Layton, Edwin T., and Roger Pineau. 1985. *And I Was There*. New York: William Morrow and Company Inc.

Lord, Walter. 1957. *Day of Infamy*. New York: Holt, Rinehart, and Winston.

Lowrey, Thomas P., and John W. G. Wellman. 1955. *The Attack on Taranto*. Mechanicsburg, Penn.: Stackpole Books.

Miller, Edward S. 1991. *War Plan Orange*. Annapolis, Md.: Naval Institute Press.

Mills, Walter. 1947. *This is Pearl! The United States and Japan –1941*. New York: William Morrow & Company.

Morgenstern, George. 1947. *Pearl Harbor: The Story of the Secret War*. New York: The Devin-Adair Company.

Morison, Samuel E. 1948. *Rising Sun in the Pacific*. Vol. 3 of *History of United States Naval Operations in World War II*. Boston: Little, Brown & Company.

Porteus, Stanley D. 1947. *Blow Not the Trumpet: A Prelude to Peril*. Palo Alto, Calif.: Pacific Books.

Prange, Gordon W.; Donald M. Goldstein; and Katherine V. Dillon. 1981. *At Dawn We Slept*. New York: McGraw-Hill.

Prange, Gordon W.; Donald M. Goldstein; and Katherine V. Dillon. 1986. *Pearl Harbor: The Final Judgment*, New York: McGraw-Hill.

Price, Willard. 1944. *Japan's Islands of Mystery*. New York: The John Day Company.

Schuler, Frank, and Robin Moore. 1976. *The Pearl Harbor Cover-Up*. New York: Pinnacle Books.

Sherrod, Robert. 1952. *History of Marine Corps Aviation in World War II*. Washington: Combat Forces Press.

Stinnett, Robert B. 2000. *Day of Deceit: The Truth about FDR and Pearl Harbor*. New York: The Free Press.

Theobald, Robert A. 1954. *The Final Secret of Pearl Harbor*. New York: The Devin-Adair Company.

Toland, John. 1977. *The Rising Sun: The Decline and Fall of the Japanese Empire 1936–1945*. New York: Random House.

United States Strategic Bombing Survey. 1946. *The Campaigns of the Pacific War*: Washington: U.S. Government Printing Office.

Weintraub, Stanley. 1991. *Long Days Journey Into War, 7 December 1941*. New York: Dutton.

Wohlstetter, Roberta. 1962. *Pearl Harbor: Warning and Decision*: Stanford, Calif.: Stanford University Press.

Worth, Roland H. 2001. *Secret Allies in the Pacific*. Jefferson, N. C.: McFarland and Company.

Index

Admiral Husband E. Kimmel was commander in chief of the Pacific Fleet
on 7 December 1941. *National Archives*

Lieutenant General Walter C. Short commanded the Hawaiian
Department of the U.S. Army on 7 December 1941. *Signal Corps*

In this rare photo, key Hawaiian commanders gather during Captain Lord Louis Mountbatten's visit in September 1941. From to left to right: (front row) Lieutenant General Walter C. Short, Mountbatten, Admiral Husband E. Kimmel, (back row) Major General Frederick L. Martin, and Rear Admiral Patrick N. L. Bellinger. *Signal Corps/National Archives*

Major General Charles D. Herron (holding the riding crop), commander of the Hawaiian Department, performs a classic peacetime inspection of Wheeler Field in 1939. The civilian to his right is Charles Edison, secretary of the navy. Next to Edison is Major Kenneth Walker, then of the 18th Pursuit Group. Walker was killed in action while leading a 1943 bombing raid in the southwest Pacific. For this effort, he was awarded a posthumous Medal of Honor. The officer second from the right in line is Bruce Holloway, who would later become a World War II fighter ace and a four-star general. Lieutenant Kenneth Bergquist is third from the right. *K. P. Bergquist*

Major General Frederick L. Martin commanded the army's Hawaiian Air Force at the time of the Japanese attack on Oahu. He was one of the architects of the Hawaiian air defense strategy but was lax and indecisive in pushing the development of the Aircraft Warning Service. At a time when the navy felt that its long-range patrol wings were being overworked, Martin did nothing to utilize his long-range bombers to alleviate the problem. *National Archives*

Brigadier General Howard C. Davidson commanded the 14th Pursuit Wing at Wheeler Field, Oahu. The Air Warning Service was under his control, and he assigned several diligent junior officers to further its establishment. But at a critical point in the manning of the information center, Davidson was in California. *National Archives*

Rear Admiral Claude C. Bloch, commanding the 14th Naval District, was in charge of all navy installations on Oahu. He failed to cooperate with the Aircraft Warning Service by ignoring or underestimating the need for a series of navy watch officers at the information center and the importance of coordinating navy-army antiaircraft batteries. *Norman Polmar*

Major Lorry N. Tindal was the first member of the Hawaiian Air Force to be schooled in the art of airborne interception. As a result, he became the first controller at the Aircraft Warning Service information center on Oahu. He reached the information center soon after the Japanese attack began and directed Army Air Force fighters as they became airborne on 7 December 1941. He testified that the Aircraft Warning Service developed slowly because of a lack of support from the Hawaiian Department. In subsequent World War II service, he was decorated for coordinating air support on D-Day during the invasion of France. *Laura Tindal Hulett*

Major Kenneth P. Bergquist was one of the young Army Air Force officers assigned to build the Air Warning Service on Oahu. A pursuit pilot, he worked diligently at the task, although he was frustrated by a lack of cooperation by senior army and navy officers. On the afternoon prior to the attack on Oahu, when the rest of the Hawaiian Air Force had the day off, Bergquist was airborne calibrating his radar stations. He later distinguished himself in the Pacific air war and rose to the rank of major general. *National Archives*

Shown with a Sikorsky OA-8 (military version of the S-43) are (left to right) Air Force Major Ken Bergquist, Corps of Engineers Major P. J. Fleming, and Signal Corps Lieutenant Colonel Carroll A. Powell. This aircraft surveyed locations for radar sites and calibrated the radar after it was operational. *W. H. Tetley*

Captain Wilfred H. Tetley, who later became a colonel, helped steer the establishment of the radar and information center of Oahu's Aircraft Warning Service. He worked closely with AAF officers Tindal and Bergquist in creating the system that was nominally operational some 10 weeks prior to the attack. *Richard Tetley*

During the summer of 1941, Wilfred H. Tetley (crouching left), Kenneth P. Bergquist (crouching right), and a survey crew established a site for a SCR-270B mobile radar unit in the Koolau Mountains on Oahu. *W. H. Tetley*

The sole navy officer on Oahu who seemed to have an understanding of the importance of the Oahu Aircraft Warning Service, and labored to get it operational, was Lieutenant Commander William E. G. Taylor. Taylor, who later became a captain, is shown here wearing a Mae West life preserver near his RAF Hawker Hurricane fighter in 1940. After the attack, he testified that the lack of cooperation from every level of the navy command was a reason Pearl Harbor was left defenseless. *Norman Polmar*

Brigadier General Jacob H. Rudolph commanded Hawaii's 18th Bomb Wing in 1941. He did not ensure that the information center was staffed properly, nor did he assist in a long-range search with his bomber aircraft. *National Archives*

Colonel William J. Flood was the commanding officer at Wheeler Field on 7 December 1941. In the absence of Brigadier General Davidson, Wheeler challenged Major General Martin's order removing 14th Pursuit Wing fighters from the protection of defensive bunkers to bunch them on the Wheeler hangar line. The assembled fighter force suffered heavy destruction, and the damage lined up on ramp. *Author's collection*

First Lieutenant Lew Sanders, commanding officer of the 46th Pursuit Squadron, led a four-plane flight of P-36s from Wheeler Field during the Japanese attack. He engaged a number of enemy aircraft near Kaneohe Bay, downing one and damaging two others. Later in the war, Sanders commanded a fighter group in the western Pacific. *Author's collection*

First Lieutenant Kermit A. Tyler drew the early watch at the information center on Sunday, 7 December 1941. Various investigative committees chastised him for failing to respond to the early radar contacts that turned out to be Japanese aircraft approaching Oahu. General Short, in his own defense, laid blame on Tyler. But the lone pursuit officer had no way of identifying the radar contacts because the center was not staffed with liaison officers. *Kermit Tyler*

Kermit Tyler (standing second from the right) later led the 44th Fighter Squadron to Guadalcanal and distinguished himself. He retired from the air force as a lieutenant colonel. *Author's collection*

Second Lieutenant George A. Whiteman, a pilot in the 44th Pursuit Squadron stationed at Bellows Field, rose to meet the Japanese attack on 7 December 1941. When strafing Zeros shot him down, he crashed and was killed. *Gayle Kent*

First Lieutenant Sam Bishop, one of the fighter pilots stationed at Bellows Field, defended against the Japanese attack and was immediately shot down, crash-landing in the surf off Bellows Field. Though wounded, he swam to shore. *USAF*

Another one of the Bellows Field officers who attempted to engage the Japanese was Second Lieutenant Hans C. Christiansen. Strafing Japanese fighters killed him next to his P-40B. *Author's collection*

John Dains was one of the young 47th Pursuit Squadron pilots who drove to Haleiwa Airfield after Wheeler Field came under attack. He flew two lone sorties in his P-40B and is believed to have shot down one enemy aircraft northeast of Oahu. Later in the morning, as he flew a P-36 from Haleiwa to Wheeler, jumpy soldiers at Schofield Barracks shot him down and killed him. *Illinois State Historical Library*

The first two Wheeler Field pilots to reach Haleiwa and mount their P-40s were Ken Taylor (left) and George Welch, both second lieutenants. They flew two sorties on 7 December 1941 that resulted in the destruction of six Japanese bombers. They both were awarded the Distinguished Service Cross. *Author's collection*

Second Lieutenant Phil Rasmussen scrambled from Wheeler Field and engaged Japanese attackers near Kaneohe Bay. Rasmussen downed a Val, but his aircraft was attacked by a Zero. Despite severe damage (some 400-plus holes) to his P-36, he returned to Wheeler. This view shows just a portion of the damage the Japanese machine guns and cannons caused. *Phil Rasmussen*

Second Lieutenant Gordon Sterling also was able to engage the enemy over Kaneohe Bay. He was killed in action during a dogfight with Japanese Zeroes. *John Sterling*

First Lieutenant John Thacker was a member of Sanders' four-plane flight from Wheeler Field. As the P-36s engaged the Japanese over Kaneohe Bay, Thacker's guns jammed, and he was had to make dangerous and frustrating dry runs at Zeroes. Early in 1944, as the commanding officer of the 46th Fighter Squadron, he exacted his revenge, downing a twin-engine Mitsubishi Betty bomber over the Marshall Islands. He is shown here with his P-39Q in the South Pacific. *Author's collection*

Second Lieutenant Harry Brown (shown in a P-36) drove to Haleiwa from Wheeler with lieutenants Bob Rogers and John Dains. He sortied with Rogers and engaged a stream of Japanese traffic near Kaena Point, downing two enemy aircraft. *Author's collection*

Bob Rogers (right), shown here late in World War II, scored a probable victory over a Japanese Val on 7 December 1941. His P-36 was hit by return fire but he landed safely at Haleiwa. He later served with the Seventh Fighter Command on Iwo Jima and flew several long-range missions over Japan. He has the distinction of flying combat sorties on both the first and last days of the Pacific war. *Author's collection*

In the year before the Japanese attack on Pearl Harbor, little Boeing P-26 fighters still made up a bulk of the aerial defense of Oahu. The fuselage stripe marks this P-26 as the personal aircraft of the 19th Squadron's commanding officer. After recognizing that Oahu's defenses were dependent on these obsolete aircraft, Army Chief of Staff General George Marshall pushed for the use of newer fighters. *Author's collection*

Although slow, inadequately armed, and ungainly, the long-range Consolidated Catalina flying boat was a reliable aircraft that operated in the Pacific throughout the war. On 7 December 1941, more than 60 were available on Oahu, but none were engaged in distant searches. Seen here is a PBY-5 model. *Stan Cohen*

Workers finish construction of the Aircraft Warning Service (AWS) information center at Fort Shafter, Oahu, in the summer of 1941. This building was patterned after similar battle-tested Royal Air Force facilities. The design featured a balcony that liaison officers used to observe the giant plotting boards on the lower level. *Author's collection*

The plotting board at the information center of the Oahu Air Warning Service at Fort Shafter is seen in here. Personnel set the radar targets, represented by wooden arrows, and moved them to represent the direction of the target's flight. Liaison officers in a balcony above the plotting board had to make an instant identification of the plots or the planes were considered hostile. The women volunteers (seen here) replaced air force technicians at the information center on 1 February 1942, freeing the men for air defense duties in more advanced locations. *Author's collection*

The radar antenna and base are seen in these two photos. *W. H. Tetley*

In 1940, only a handful of Curtiss P-36 Hawks were in Hawaii. Above: Curtiss Hawk fighters of the 6th Pursuit Squadron on the Wheeler Field ramp. Below: P-36As of the 78th Pursuit Squadron at Bellows Field for gunnery training in 1941. After those in Washington began to worry about Hawaiian defenses, 30 Hawks, drawn from stateside units, were ferried to Oahu in February 1941. *Author's collection*

The Douglas B-18, shown above at Wheeler Field and below in a formation near Oahu, was a mainstay in the Hawaiian Air Force's Bomber Command. Thirty-three were in inventory on 7 December 1941 and 21 of these were available for reconnaissance up to 500 miles. However, based on command decisions, they remained on the ground in the critical days before the Japanese attack. Twelve were destroyed at Hickam Filed during the attack. *Sam Smith*

Inside the mobile van of a SCR-270B radar unit, an operator manipulates the controls and observes the echo, or radar return, on the oscilloscope. *W. H. Tetley*

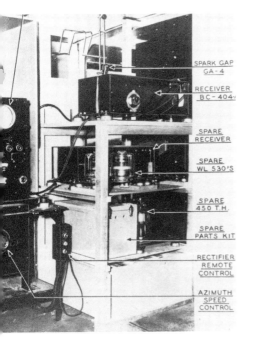

SPARK GAP
GA-4

RECEIVER
BC-404

SPARE
RECEIVER

SPARE
WL 530'S

SPARE
450 T.H.

SPARE
PARTS KIT

RECTIFIER
REMOTE
CONTROL

AZIMUTH
SPEED
CONTROL

Some of the equipment in the van of a SCR-270B radar unit. *W. H. Tetley*

While the Hawaiian command disdained using its Douglas B-18s for a long-range search or for anti-submarine missions, the aircraft were being employed in exactly that role in December 1941.

Above: An Army Air Force B-18A at a Caribbean air base. *USAF*

Below: A Canadian B-18 sub-hunting over the Atlantic. *National Archives of Canada*

The navy believed that it had too few PBYs to use on search missions from Oahu and contended that those aircraft were the only ones it had with long-range capabilities. However, the navy and marines possessed 12 Sikorsky JRS-1 amphibian transports at Ford Island with a range of 378 nautical miles. No one considered using these aircraft to augment the patrol squadrons' search missions until after the attack. After the initial strike, a pair of the unarmed JRS-1 aircraft was launched to search for the enemy task force. One from VJ-1 patrolled far enough north to encounter and escape Zeroes protecting the Japanese carrier force. Shown here is a post-attack JRS-1 that had been outfitted for anti-submarine work.
National Archives

The North American O-47's construction reflected the U.S. Army prewar doctrine that Army Air Corps missions were used to support ground forces. Several of these large aircraft, which were virtually useless to the Hawaiian army in the limited confines of Oahu, could have conducted submarine patrols near the Pearl Harbor approaches. This would have allowed for some army and navy reconnaissance of distant areas. However, this cooperative arrangement did not occur during the hours preceding the Pearl Harbor attack. *Author's collection*

As a part of the Hawaiian defense expansion, considerable antiaircraft artillery was supplied to General Short's command on Oahu. By December 1941, 98 heavy antiaircraft guns were counted in the army inventory.

Right: The Oahu populous inspects a mobile three-inch gun on Army Day, April 1941. Below: Acoustical sound locators served several of the heavy antiaircraft batteries. *Author's collection*

Mechanics unbutton a new P-40B Tomahawk at Bellows Field in preparation for bore sighting its six machine guns. *Sam Smith*

Curtiss P-40B Tomahawk fighters of the 19th Pursuit Squadron, 18th Pursuit Group are shown in flight a few days before the Japanese attack. Of the 99 P-40B and P-40C aircraft in the Hawaiian Air Force inventory prior to the attack, 42 were destroyed. Bombs and strafing demolished 40 of them while two were ruined in aerial combat. *Gus Ahola*

Forty Nakajima Kate's, like this one carrying 800 kilogram torpedoes slung beneath the fuselage, caused chaos among the warships along Battleship Row off Ford Island, Pearl Harbor. The Nakajima B5N Kate (also pictured below) of the Japanese navy carried either a torpedo or armor-piercing bomb. Kates were relatively slow, particularly when laden with ordnance, and would have been easy picking for Army Air Force fighters. But by the time the few P-36s and P-40s that got into the fight encountered the Kates, they had already attacked their intended targets. *National Archives*

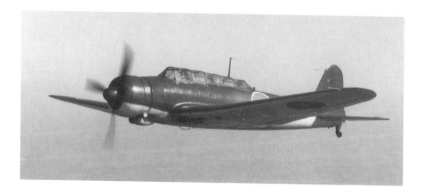

The Japanese carrier strike force sent a pair of Aichi E13A1 Jakes ahead of its air groups to survey Lahina Roads and Pearl Harbor. Radar detected them, but no liaison officers were manning the information center so that the early intruders could be identified. *National Defense College, Tokyo*

The aircraft carrier *Shokaku*'s B5N Kate bombers warm their engines prior to departure for Oahu as a last A6M Zero fighter (foreground) prepares to launch for combat air patrol over the Japanese fleet. *National Archives*

The Japanese did not target Haleiwa airstrip on the north coast of Oahu. The 47th Pursuit Squadron had gone there a few days before the attack, and its fighters were manned by several squadron members who drove from Wheeler Field on their own initiative to engage the enemy. *National Archives*

Following Page:

This aerial view (looking south) of Pearl Harbor taken on 30 October 1941 clearly shows some of the main targets of the Japanese raid on 7 December 1941. Ford Island is in the center of the harbor. On this day five battleships and the aircraft carrier *Lexington* are moored nearby. Cruisers, destroyers, and various auxiliary vessels are anchored north of the island. About 20 PBYs are visible at the air station. Hickam Field lies just south of Ford Island, past some fuel storage tanks and adjacent to the entrance channel. *U.S. Navy, National Archives*

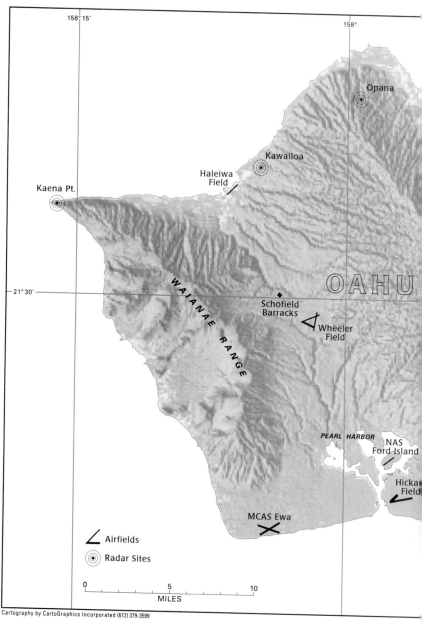

158° 15'

158°

Opana

Kawailoa

Haleiwa
Field

Kaena Pt.

21° 30'

WAIANAE RANGE

OAHU

Schofield
Barracks

Wheeler
Field

PEARL HARBOR   NAS
Ford Island

Hicka
Field

MCAS Ewa

∠ Airfields

⊙ Radar Sites

0   5   10
MILES

Cartography by CartoGraphics Incorporated (612) 379-3599

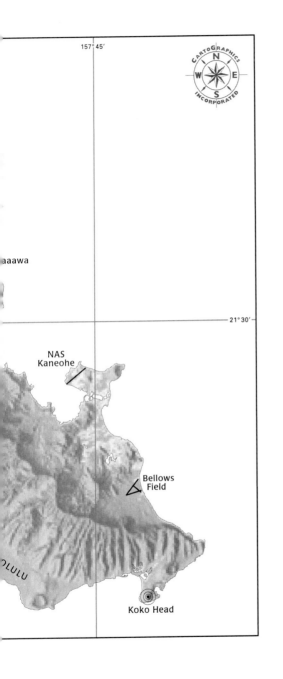

As of 7 December 1941 the Island of Oahu, Hawaii, was home to the military installations and radar sites shown here.

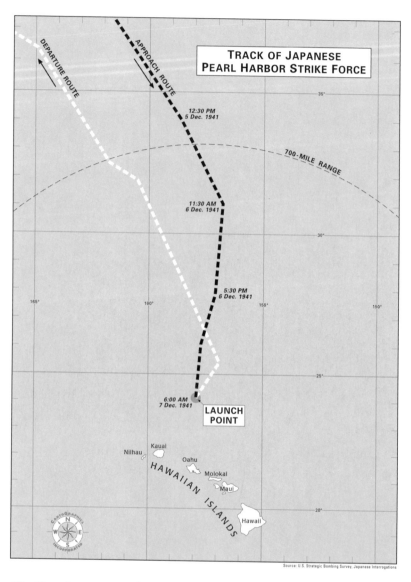

TRACK OF JAPANESE PEARL HARBOR STRIKE FORCE

DEPARTURE ROUTE

APPROACH ROUTE

35°

700-MILE RANGE

12:30 PM
5 Dec. 1941

11:30 AM
6 Dec. 1941

30°

5:30 PM
6 Dec. 1941

165°   160°   155°   150°

25°

6:00 AM
7 Dec. 1941

LAUNCH POINT

Kauai
Niihau
Oahu
HAWAIIAN
Molokai
Maui
ISLANDS
20°

Hawaii

N W E S

CARTOGRAPHIC INCORPORATED

Source: U.S. Strategic Bombing Survey, Japanese Interrogations

The Hawaiian command structure maintained that it did not have sufficient long-range aircraft to conduct distant search missions that might have alerted Oahu. Facts suggest otherwise. While some of the Japanese fleet's approach was during hours of darkness, long-range searches within the 700-mile range limit of U.S. Navy and Army Air Force aircraft might have detected either the 20-ship Japanese surface armada or its 183-plane first wave of aircraft. No search missions were flown from 5 December onward.

A Curtiss P-40s burns at Wheeler Field after the Japanese attack. This is one was destroyed on the ground. *Author's collection*

An aerial view of Ford Island taken from a Japanese aircraft just after the first wave attack began. A Japanese D3A Val is visible low over Battleship Row. *National Archives*

An Aichi D3A Val of the Zuikaku air group returns from the Pearl Harbor attack. *National Defense College, Tokyo*

Following Page:

Japanese dive bombers from the aircraft carrier *Zuikaku* caused widespread destruction at Wheeler Field. First they hit the neat rows of fighter planes lining the ramp, igniting fuel that sent columns of smoke skyward. Then they concentrated on hangars and other buildings. Three D3A Vals are visible in this Japanese photo. *National Archives*

ホイラー飛行場を爆撃す
の直前に並べられたP-40
ている。画面中央から道
、爆撃する99艦爆、中央
軍機左転中の1機が見える

Type 99 Carrier Bombers (D3A1, Val) of Carrier ZUIKAKU raid Wheeler Airfield, Hawaii, Dec. 8, 1941. (Photo: H. Yaegashi)

A view of Battleship Row taken from a horizontal bomber during the attack of 7 December 1941. At the bottom of the photo are the *Oklahoma* and the *Maryland* (nearest to Ford Island). Note that the *Oklahoma* has already begun to role over on her port side from several torpedo hits. She will eventually capsize. Next in line are the *West Virginia*, beginning to settle, and the *Tennessee* (nearest Ford Island). The next two are the repair ship *Vestal* and the battleship *Arizona* (nearest Ford Island). Last in line alone is the *Nevada*, partially obscured by smoke. Torpedoes have hit all of the outboard ships, which now are hemorrhaging fuel oil. *National Archives*

The battleship *Arizona* was struck first by several bombs, one of which touched off her forward magazine. Although she already has settled to the bottom in this view, the ship still burns. Her foremast and bridge have collapsed to a 45-degree angle. The damage was so severe that she could not be repaired. Her hull remains underwater to this day as a memorial to the fallen. *U.S. Navy, National Archives*

The first wave of attacking Japanese aircraft achieved complete surprise and for a few minutes dove on their targets without opposition. By the time that the second wave of Japanese attackers appeared over Pearl Harbor, the sky was a cauldron of smoke and exploding antiaircraft fire. The smoke column (center) is from the *Arizona*. *U.S. Navy, National Archives*

Following Page:
Three bombs hit the destroyer *Shaw* as it was in floating dry dock at the shipyard. Fires eventually reached her main magazine causing this massive explosion. *U.S. Navy, National Archives*

Previous Page:

Although damaged in the initial attack, the battleship *Nevada* managed to get underway from her mooring off Ford Island and began a run to the open sea. However, Lieutenant Commander Mitsuo Fuchida, the leader of the Japanese strike force, then directed several of his bombers toward the great warship, and subsequent hits caused concern that she would sink and block the channel. Here, the wounded *Nevada* can be seen as she is grounded off Hospital Point. The seaplane tender *Avocet* is moored in the foreground. *National Archives*

All three ships berthed in dry dock No.1 at the time of the attack received bomb hits. The battleship *Pennsylvania* (background) shrugged off her damage, but the destroyers *Downes* (left, foreground) and *Cassin* (capsized on the right) were damaged so severely that they had to be completely rebuilt with new hulls and some salvaged machinery. *U.S. Navy, National Archives*

A Val, on fire from being hit by a ship's batteries, plunges to its death over Pearl Harbor. *National Archives*

A Val, with its dive brakes still extended and bomb gone, pulls out of its attack on the U.S. Pacific Fleet at Pearl Harbor. *National Archives*

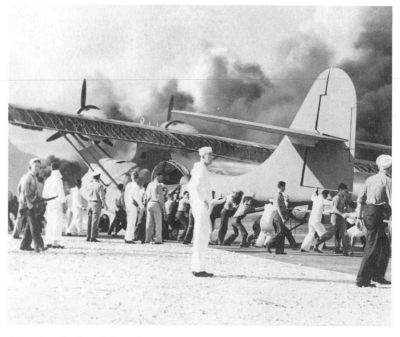

A horde of sailors labored to save a few PBYs from the fires caused by the attack on Kaneohe Naval Air Station. This one PBY had its fabric control surfaces burned but seems otherwise intact. *U.S. Navy, National Archives*